DESIGNING
QUALITATIVE
RESEARCH

DESIGNING QUALITATIVE RESEARCH

SECOND EDITION

CATHERINE MARSHALL
GRETCHEN B. ROSSMAN

SAGE Publications
International Educational and Professional Publisher
Thousand Oaks   London   New Delhi

For information address:

SAGE Publications, Inc.
2455 Teller Road
Thousand Oaks, California 91320

SAGE Publications Ltd.
6 Bonhill Street
London EC2A 4PU
United Kingdom

SAGE Publications India Pvt. Ltd.
M-32 Market
Greater Kailash I
New Delhi 110 048 India

Printed in the United States of America

Library of Congress Cataloging-in-Publication Data

Marshall, Catherine.
    Designing qualitative research / Catherine Marshall, Gretchen B. Rossman.—2nd ed.
        p.   cm.
    Includes bibliographical references and index.
    ISBN 0-8039-5248-1.—ISBN 0-8039-5249-X (pbk.)
        1. Social sciences—Research—Methodology.   I. Rossman, Gretchen B.   II. Title.
    H62.M277   1994
    300'.72—dc20   94-31048

95 96 97 98 99 10 9 8 7 6 5 4 3 2 1

Sage Production Editor: Astrid Virding

Contents

Preface to the Second Edition

The first edition of this book was designed to fill a need. The need? That many of our doctoral students had few useful, comprehensive texts to guide them through the difficult, tedious, and exciting process of developing a qualitative research proposal. Many exemplary texts on qualitative methods existed then; even more do so now. We wanted to provide practical assistance through the processes of designing that research. Now, however, we find that the discourse in methodology has changed substantially. What seemed clear-cut and precise in 1989 is no longer so. We have both learned about the messiness and complexity of designing research, moreover, as we have guided students through the proposal design process. This edition of *Designing Qualitative Research,* then, is an essential revision of the earlier work.

Qualitative research is evolving, through intellectual, political, and even technological struggles and advances. Critical theorists and feminists demonstrate that openly ideological or value-explicit stances in research are essential for identifying the political assumptions embedded in our social institutions. The management of large databases has become possible with sophisticated software. The second edition retains the original purpose—

that of providing a clear, hands-on guide, a "how-to" book for those who wish to design qualitative research, and do so with sensitivity to the subtleties and complexities that current political, ethical, and technological thinking suggest. Established researchers, graduate students, program managers, planners, and policy analysts will find this second edition useful in thinking through the facets of a solid research proposal. Although many of the examples are from education, social scientists from a number of disciplines should find the text helpful. In fact, over the years, students from management, urban planning, sociology, psychology, communications, and social work have taken our courses based on this book.

The students we have had the privilege to work with over the years have shaped our thinking about qualitative research; their influence is present throughout this second edition, as many are cited throughout the text. These individuals have asked deep questions that challenged both of us to reframe and expand on the book, hopefully making it clearer, more interdisciplinary, and relevant to wider audiences. In particular, we gratefully acknowledge the work of students reflected in Chapter 4; the detailed descriptions and bibliographic references have been generated, in large part, by students in our courses. The sections on Focus Group Interviewing and Phenomenological Interviewing were written by Dara Tomlin Rossman, Gretchen's older daughter, who also provided stylistic editing of the book and bibliographic editing; her work has been thorough and precise, and her contributions are greatly appreciated.

We also want to acknowledge Mitch Allen's guiding influence. At his urging, we made sure that the first edition would appeal across a range of disciplines. Later, again at his urging, we pressed forward with the second edition with the knowledge that new developments in qualitative methodology demanded revisions in the original work. In addition, we appreciate the personal letters and published reviews of the first edition, and the helpful comments and suggestions of David Evans, Julianne Salzman, and Elise Litterick on this edition.

We hope this second edition will continue to be the practical guide that the first edition has proven to be in helping researchers craft sound, thoughtful, and sensitive qualitative research proposals.

1 Introduction

Qualitative research methods have become increasingly important modes of inquiry for the social sciences and applied fields such as education, regional planning, and management. Long dominated by methods borrowed from the experimental sciences, the social sciences now present a sometimes confusing array of appropriate alternative research methods. From anthropology come ethnomethodology and ethnoscience, as well as the more familiar ethnography. Sociology has yielded symbolic interactionism and the Chicago School. The philosophers would have us engage in concept analysis, and interdisciplinary work has spawned sociolinguistics, discourse analysis, life histories, and clinical methodology. The critical traditions bring feminist research and critical ethnography, as well as action and participatory research, all intended to radically change fundamental social structures and processes and to reconceptualize the entire research enterprise.

Clearly, with such wide-ranging intellectual roots, qualitative research needs some generally recognized common procedures. This book is intended to be a guide to researchers who have chosen some variety of qualitative methods as a means to better understand, and perhaps change, a complex social phenomenon. Throughout the text we refer to *qualitative research* and *qualitative methods* as if these were one agreed-upon set that everyone understands; we intend no such implication.

Jacob (1987, 1988) has categorized qualitative research traditions in education. Drawing on discipline bases and historical traditions, she identifies six major domains. First is *human ethology,* represented by the work of Blurton-Jones (1972) and Smith (1974). This approach seeks to understand the range of behaviors in which people naturally engage. Data are gathered through observation (sometimes recorded on videotape) and analyzed quantitatively.

The next domain is *ecological psychology,* which stresses the interaction of the person and environment in shaping behavior. Based on the work of Barker (1968) and Lewin (1936), ecological psychology also relies on observational data, supplemented with specimen records. The environment is especially important. As Day, Perkins, and Weinthaler (1979) note, "The physical setting, its characteristics and arrangement, both suggest and inhibit behavior" (p. 3). Describing these behaviors and analyzing the influence of the environment on them are the primary goals of this approach.

Holistic ethnography, as seen in the work of Goodenough (1971), Mead (1970), and Sanday (1979), is the third domain or tradition. Here, human culture is a crucial concept, one that researchers in this tradition try to describe and analyze fully. Employing participant observation as a primary approach to gathering data, holistic ethnographers try to uncover and document participants' perspectives.

Cognitive anthropologists assume that participants' perspectives are organized into cognitive or semantic schemata-categories of meaning that are systematically related to one another. Spradley (1979) describes how data are gathered through in-depth interviewing and then analyzed qualitatively to identify domains of understanding.

The work of Erickson (1977) and his colleagues (Erickson & Mahatt, 1982; Erickson & Wilson, 1982) exemplifies *ethnography of communication,* Jacob's (1988) fifth domain. Drawing heavily on linguistics, these ethnographers gather data about verbal and nonverbal interactions, relying on participant observation and audio- or videotape of these interactions.

The sixth domain is *symbolic interactionism,* represented in the work of Blumer (1969) and Denzin (1978). Here the research interest is in understanding how individuals take and make meaning in interaction with others. The emphasis is on the pressures of meaning-making in social organization.

Soundly critiqued by three British methodologists (Atkinson, Delamont, & Hammersley, 1988) as ethnocentric and as ill-advisedly relying on "Kuhnian models," Jacob's typology was greatly enhanced by their contributions. Noting that there is some overlap in the types listed but presenting the work of British qualitative researchers as exemplars, Atkinson et al. (1988) describe seven approaches to qualitative research: symbolic interactionism, anthropology, sociolinguistics, ethnomethodology, democratic evaluation, neo-Marxist ethnography, and feminism. Of these, the most distinctive from Jacob's are ethnomethodology, democratic evaluation, neo-Marxist and critical ethnography, and feminism.

Practitioners of *ethnomethodology,* which is closely allied to the discourse analysis of sociolinguists, conceptualize classrooms, for example, as speech-exchange systems and strive to understand the "interactional management of classroom knowledge" (Atkinson et al., 1988, p. 239). The works of Hammersley (1977) and Hargreaves (1984) focus on how hard students have to work to understand teachers' questions in order to produce acceptable responses (Atkinson et al., 1988).

In recent years, some qualitative researchers have abandoned the pretense of neutrality and developed research that is openly ideological and has an empowering and democratizing purpose. The following four traditions represent this newer perspective that takes as a fundamental purpose the critique of existing social structures and relations.

Democratic evaluation evolved as disillusion with quantitative methods for evaluating curricula grew, coupled with a rejection of the authoritarian notion that an outsider should evaluate a teacher's work. Arguing that the evaluator should be a facilitator, this approach experimented with a variety of qualitative methods (see Walker, 1983).

Neo-Marxist ethnography, or *critical ethnography,* developed from a commitment to radical schooling that found expression in several works sharply critical of accepted teaching practice (Keddie, 1971; Sharp & Green, 1975; Young, 1971). Later work of this type focused on the constraints on the adoption of radical teaching practices (Atkinson et al., 1988). Anderson (1989) and Marshall (1991) demonstrate how critical ethnography can go beyond the classroom to ask questions about fundamental policy, power, and dominance issues and dilemmas in schooling, including the role of the school in reproducing gender, race, and other social inequities.

Feminist research fits no accepted tradition outlined by Jacob (1988) but relies on qualitative methods and "draw[s] . . . inspiration from feminism"

(Atkinson et al., 1988, p. 242). Studies in this genre have examined gender differences in schools (Clarricoates, 1980, 1987) as well as the development of adolescent girls (Griffin, 1985; Lees, 1986). After Harding's (1987) critique of male bias in social science, feminist research has blossomed. Lather (1991) combines feminist research and critical ethnography, advocating agendas that intend to "challenge the legitimacy of the dominant order . . . [and] turn critical thought into emancipating action" (p. xv).

To these, we would add *action research* and *participatory research*. Each has the change of existing social systems as a primary purpose, although participatory research is often more explicitly ideological, following the precepts of emancipation articulated by Friere (1970). Full collaboration between researcher and participants in posing the questions to be pursued and gathering data to respond to them is the hallmark of these approaches, and can be found in the new teacher-as-researcher strategy in education (Kemmis & McTaggert, 1982; McKernan, 1991). Participatory research is exemplified by the research of Maguire (1987) on battered women.

These typologies provide ways of categorizing some of the variety of qualitative research approaches. Each tradition assumes that systematic inquiry must occur in a natural setting rather than an artificially constrained one such as an experiment. The approaches vary, however, depending on how interactive the researcher is in gathering data, whether those data document nonverbal or verbal behavior or both, whether it is appropriate to question the participants as to how they view their worlds, and how the data can most fruitfully be analyzed.

The above discussion should give the reader some sense of the array of methods subsumed under the qualitative umbrella. This text cannot do justice to the rich variety of qualitative methods. We intend instead to describe the process of designing mainstream qualitative research that entails immersion in the everyday life of the setting chosen for study, values and seeks to discover participants' perspectives on their worlds, views inquiry as an interactive process between the researcher and the participants, is both descriptive and analytic, and relies on people's words and observable behavior as the primary data. Whether some particular methodological refinement is qualitative or not is a debate for another arena. Our purpose here is to provide practical guidance to those embarking on an exciting, sometimes frustrating, but ultimately rewarding journey into inquiry.

The evocative case study and the rich description in ethnography are the product of systematic inquiry. In their beginnings, however, they were once modest research proposals. Researchers, however, had to search hard to find few explicit guidelines for writing thorough, convincing research proposals. Some qualitative research is so lacking in focus and design description that it appears to have none; novice researchers have difficulty learning from such reports. Other research findings are presented without relating the messiness inherent in qualitative research; such versions provide no clear guidelines for those contemplating qualitative research. This book fills a need by providing *specific* guidance for writing a proposal that is grounded in the assumptions of qualitative methodology and convinces reviewers of the design soundness.

Reviewers for funding agencies, as well as dissertation committees, sometimes look askance at qualitative research proposals. Too often, proposers speak vaguely of their projected research; it seems an unfocused, unplanned desire to go out in the world and "hang out" or "muck around." This book is organized as a guide through the process of writing a qualitative research proposal, demonstrating how to write a proposal that reassures reviewers by defining explicit steps to follow, principles to adhere to, and rationales for the strengths of the qualitative approach.

Sociologists, community psychologists, criminologists, anthropologists, political scientists, regional planners, and others from a range of the social sciences and applied fields will find this guide useful. Although many of the examples come from the field of education (because of our own backgrounds), the principles, challenges, and opportunities are transferable across disciplines and into other applied fields.

This book does not replace the numerous texts, readers, and journal articles that are important for learning qualitative methodology. It is meant to complement the numerous existing texts that explicate the philosophical bases, the history, and the findings of qualitative studies. Its purpose is to give practical, useful guidance for writing proposals that fit within the qualitative paradigm and that are successful.

The Challenges

Researchers who would conduct qualitative research face at least three challenges: (1) to develop a conceptual framework for the study that is thorough, concise, and elegant; (2) to plan a design that is systematic and manageable yet flexible; and (3) to integrate these into a coherent document that convinces the proposal reader—a funding agency or a dissertation committee—that the study should be done, can be done, and will be done.

Should Do-Ability

The first challenge is to build an argument that the study will contribute to theory and research—the ongoing conversation in a particular social science discipline or applied field—and that it will be significant for policy and practice. This consideration addresses the familiar "So what?" question to which the researcher should respond cogently and knowledgeably about why the study should be conducted.

Do-Ability

The second challenge is to demonstrate the feasibility, or do-ability, of the study. This depends on judgments about sufficiency of available resources (time, money); access to the site and/or population of interest; ethical considerations; and the researcher's knowledge and skills. A discussion of resources is integral to proposals seeking external funding but just as important for dissertation research. The researcher should also discuss strategies for access to a specific site or strategies to identify participants for the study. Ethical considerations should be thoughtfully and sensitively analyzed, both generic ethical issues in qualitative research and ones specific to the site or the participants. Finally, throughout the proposal the researcher demonstrates the capability of conducting a thorough, ethical qualitative research study. In citing the methodological literature and discussing pilot studies or previous research, the researcher reveals familiarity with the ongoing methodological discourse and experience in conducting qualitative research.

Want-To-Do-Ability

In contrast, the want-to-do-ability is solely a function of the researcher's engagement in the topic. Far removed from the dispassionate scientist of the past, the qualitative researcher cares deeply about the substance of the inquiry at hand. This should not suggest that qualitative research is subjectivist and biased—all-too-common criticisms. Rather, qualitative inquiry acknowledges that all social science research may well be subjectivist and shifts the discourse to a discussion of epistemology and strategies for ensuring trustworthy and credible studies. The proposal, then, is an argument making the case that the study can and should be done, and that there is sufficient energy and interest to sustain it.

Developing an Argument

Central to this book is the premise that proposal development is a process of building an argument supporting the proposed work. Not unlike the logic of formal debate or the reasoning of a position paper, a research proposal is intended to convince the reader that the proposed work is significant, relevant, and interesting; that the design of the study is sound; and that the researcher is capable of successfully conducting the study. The proposal writer must, therefore, build a logical argument supporting the endeavor, amass evidence in support of each point, and show how the entire enterprise is integrated conceptually.

Research proposals can be thought of as having two major sections: the conceptual framework, and the design and research methods. Roughly corresponding to the "what"—the substantive focus of the inquiry—and the "how"—the means for conducting that inquiry—these two sections of the proposal detail the specific topic or issue to be explored, as well as the proposed means for that exploration. In a sound, well-developed, and well-argued proposal, the sections relate with integrity: They share common epistemological assumptions; congruence between research questions and methods chosen to explore the topic is apparent.

Conceptual Framework

The first section that demands a solid rationale is the conceptual framework of the study. In examining a specific setting or set of individuals, the writer should show how she is studying a *case* of a larger phenomenon.[1] By linking the specific research questions to larger theoretical constructs or to national policy issues, the writer shows that the particulars of the study serve to illuminate larger issues and, therefore, are of significance.

The economics doctoral student, for example, who demonstrates that his qualitative case studies of five families' financial decision making are relevant for understanding larger marketplace forces, while focusing at the individual level, has met this condition. The case studies are significant because they illuminate in detail larger economic forces.

Similarly, the university research team that designs a teacher induction project evaluation component stipulating phenomenological in-depth interviewing as the sole data collection method, and links this approach to socialization theory, has begun to build a case for the proposal that grounds it to important theoretical and empirical literatures. This logic is developed in Chapter 2.

Design Soundness

The second area for building a sound argument in favor of the proposal is its design. The writer should show that the design is the result of a series of decisions she made based on knowledge gained from the methodological literature and previous work. Justification for those decisions should derive not only from the methodological literature; it should also flow logically from the research questions and the conceptual framework surrounding those questions.

Because qualitative research proposals are at times unfamiliar to reviewers, the logic supporting the choice of those methods must be sound. Ensuring a clear, logical rationale in support of qualitative methods entails attention to seven topics: (1) the assumptions of qualitative approaches; (2) the logic for selecting a sample or participants; (3) the choice of overall design and data collection methods; (4) an acknowledgment of the intensive aspects of fieldwork; (5) a consideration of ethical issues; (6) the resource needs; and (7) attention to the trustworthiness of the overall design. The first five of these areas are considered in detail in Chapters 3, 4, and 5; the sixth, resource needs, is discussed in Chapter 6, and ensuring the trustworthiness of the study is elaborated in Chapter 7.

Researcher Competence

Finally, in developing an argument to support the proposal, the writer should explicitly and implicitly demonstrate competence. The exact standard of competence applied for evaluating the proposal depends on the purpose and scope of the research; most likely, the standards applied to a dissertation proposal will differ from those used to evaluate a multiyear funded project written by established researchers. Paradoxically, because dissertation research is intended to provide an opportunity for *becoming competent,* careful scrutiny will be given to all portions of the proposal. The dissertation proposal writer will be expected to have given thorough attention to every facet of the conceptual framework and the research design. Established researchers, on the other hand, may not receive such careful scrutiny because their record of previous work engenders trust, and the logic of good faith preserves standards of competence. Although this may seem unfair, it nevertheless reflects the reality of proposal evaluation.

Demonstrating competence, then, involves reference to the proposal writer's previous work, discussion of a pilot study's strengths and weaknesses, and discussion of the proposal writer's course work and other relevant educational experiences, as well as the overall high quality of the proposal's organization, conceptual framework, and design.

Two vignettes are presented to illuminate this process of building an argument to support qualitative research. The first describes a doctoral student in sociology trying to convince her dissertation committee that qualitative methods are best suited for exploratory research on the culture of a hospital. Her research is intended to uncover patterns in the work life of participants that will lead to important improvement in the treatment of patients. Vignette 2 shows researchers building a rationale around the strengths of qualitative methods for policy analysis. The researchers had to convince legislators that qualitative methods would yield useful, vivid analyses that could inform the policy-making process. The implications for building an argument in support of qualitative proposals are developed after the vignettes, followed by an overview of the rest of the book.

Vignette 1

Justifying Fieldwork to Explore Organizational Culture [2]

As O'Brien reviewed the notes she had written to help with the proposal defense, she realized that her strongest argument rested on two aspects of the proposed study's significance: its exploratory purpose and its commitment to improving patient treatment in large urban hospitals. She realized that the latter aspect might be construed as biased, but if she kept the rationale grounded in the need to better understand complex interactions, tacit processes, and often hidden beliefs and values, she could demonstrate the study's clear potential to improve practice.

Her committee was composed of two quantitatively trained
sociologists and a medical anthropologist. She knew she had the support
of the anthropologist, whose advice had been crucial during the several
proposal drafts she had written. The two sociologists, however, were
more likely to be critical of the design.

O'Brien decided to begin her presentation with an explication of the
four purposes of research (exploration, explanation, description, and
prediction) in order to link the purpose of her proposed study to
general principles regarding the conduct of inquiry. She could then
proceed quite logically to a discussion of the ways in which exploratory
research can serve to identify important variables for subsequent
explanatory or predictive research. This logic could allay the concerns of
the two quantitatively oriented sociologists, who would search the
proposal for testable hypotheses, instrumentation and
operationalization of variables, and tests of reliability.

The second major justification of the study would develop from its
significance for practice. O'Brien recalled how she had reviewed
empirical studies that indicated that organizational conditions had a
significant effect on wellness and hospital leaving rates. What had not
been identified in those studies were the specific interactions between
hospital staff and patients, the widely shared beliefs about patients
among the staff, and the organizational norms governing patient
treatment. Her research, she would argue, would help identify those
tacit, often hidden, aspects of organizational life.

Engaging in exploratory research where the relevant variables had not
been identified and uncovering the tacit aspects of organizational life
demanded qualitative methods. Fieldwork would be most appropriate
for discovering the relevant variables and building a thorough, rich,
detailed description of hospital culture. By linking her proposed
research to concepts familiar to the quantitative sociologists, O'Brien
hoped to draw the sociologists into the logic supporting her proposal
and to convince them of its sound design.

Quite often, a researcher's first task, even before the formulation of the
proposal, is to convince critics that the research will be useful. In many
cases, and especially in policy research, one can appeal to policy makers'
frustration with previous research. Too often, policy studies present analyses of outcomes that provide little sense of how processes created those

outcomes. The next vignette shows how two researchers convinced their superiors that they could answer pressing policy questions with qualitative methods.

Vignette 2

Convincing Policy Makers of the Utility of Qualitative Methods [2]

Why, 6 months after state legislators had allocated $10 million to provide temporary shelters, were homeless families still sleeping in cars? Keppel and Wilson, researchers in the legislative analyst's office, knew that the question begged for qualitative research methodology. Their challenge would be to convince their superiors that the qualitative approach, although more time-consuming than a survey, was the better way to go.

They prepared the following memo:

Memorandum Regarding Homeless Family Shelter Policy

This memo is to explain the general usefulness of qualitative research for answering policy questions. At tomorrow's meeting, we will show you how this general discussion applies to the analysis of the Homeless Family Shelter Policy.

We know that you and your colleagues have been, at various times, frustrated with studies and evaluations that tell you the outcomes only after things have already gone wrong. In complex policy arenas, like homelessness, we believe that you need information to help you understand the problem, identify areas you can influence, and see the consequences of policy intervention in real life. You can do little with studies that tell you that policies have had little or no effect. In addition, we believe that you need information that will enable you to see beyond simple dependent variables. Thus we believe that this agency's approach to policy analysis ought to include qualitative research methods. We believe that benefits for you in formulating policy include the following:

1. qualitative methods identify and describe the complexity of social problems like homelessness,
2. qualitative methods identify the unanticipated outcomes of policies,

3. qualitative methods help "debug" policy—they find inconsistencies and conflicts built into policies,

4. qualitative methods identify how policies are changed as they are implemented in various levels,

5. qualitative methods help find the "natural" solutions to problems—the solutions that people devise without policy intervention, and

6. qualitative methods provide a way to study problems in cases where experiments would be unethical (Marshall, 1987).

We hope that you will give us the opportunity to demonstrate the viability of qualitative research and to build the capacity of the legislative analyst's office in that direction. Too often, our research and evaluations miss the mark. It is far better to have an approximate answer to the right question than an exact answer to the wrong question. We look forward to tomorrow's discussion.

In their 30-minute discussion, Keppel and Wilson built their argument around two major points. The first was that there are numerous implementation questions concerning homelessness to be explored in the real-world setting; the second, that certain subtleties of the policy implementation process had to be explored to understand fully what was happening.

Keppel and Wilson's strategy called for visiting shelters and implementing agents, and interviewing members of homeless families, with the intent of uncovering the complex interactions of bureaucracy, money, implementing agents' goals and motivations, and local site interpretation of policy and homeless family situations. The immediate goal was the discovery of the right questions to ask, followed by the systematic collection of data. Keppel and Wilson convinced their superiors that their findings would help make clear the important questions, describe patterns of implementation, and identify the challenges and barriers that could lead to more effective policy outcomes.

In Vignette 2 we see researchers convincing others that a qualitative study is needed. This underscores the notion that researchers proposing qualitative inquiry do best by emphasizing the promise of quality, depth, and richness in the findings. They may, however, encounter puzzlement and resistance from those accustomed to experimental research; they may need to translate between qualitative and quantitative paradigms. Researchers who are convinced that a qualitative approach is best for the question or problem at hand should make a case that "thick description" (Geertz, 1973, p. 5) and systematic and detailed analysis will yield valuable explorations and explanations of processes.

Overview of the Book

The remainder of the book takes the reader through the sections of a qualitative research proposal. Chapter 2 discusses the complex task of building a conceptual framework around the study. Such a process entails moving beyond the initial puzzle or intriguing paradox and embedding it in appropriate traditions of research; it links the specific case to larger theoretical domains. This argument also should demonstrate the proposed study's significance to larger social policy issues and to the everyday lives of people. Thus the study's general focus and research questions, related literature, and significance are interrelated aspects of the conceptual framework. We call this the substance of the study—the "what."

Chapter 3 presents a detailed discussion of the "how" of the study. Having focused on a research problem with a set of questions or a domain to explore, the proposal should then describe how systematic inquiry will yield data that will respond to the questions. The proposer should discuss the logic and assumptions of the overall design and methods, linking these directly to the focus of the study. Here the choice of qualitative methods should be justified.

Chapter 4 describes primary and secondary data collection methods. This chapter is not intended to replace the many exemplary texts that deal in great detail with methods; rather, we present a brief discussion of various alternatives and their strengths and weaknesses. Chapter 5 then describes procedures for managing, recording, and analyzing qualitative data. Here, the discussion focuses on considerations at the proposal stage.

Chapter 6 describes the complex, iterative process of projecting the resources necessary for the study. Time, personnel, and financial resources should be considered. Finally, Chapter 7 revisits the notion introduced here of the proposal as an argument. Criteria for evaluating the soundness and competence of a qualitative proposal are discussed, with special attention to building a logical rationale and answering challenges from critics.

Throughout the book we use vignettes to illustrate the points being made. Most of these are drawn from our own work and that of other social scientists. Where a vignette is fictitious, we identify it as such (see Note 2). The vignettes vary considerably in length, depending on the level of detail needed to illustrate the point. Many are from the field of education, reflecting our own backgrounds. We feel that the principles depicted in the vignettes are applicable to research grounded in several disciplines as well as applied fields.

Two themes run through this book. *Design flexibility* is a crucial feature of qualitative inquiry; demands for specificity in design and method selection, however, seem to preclude such flexibility. We urge the researcher to think of the proposal as an initial plan; one that is thorough, sound, well thought out, and based on current knowledge. The proposal reveals sensitivity to the setting, the issues to be explored, and the ethical dilemmas sure to be encountered, but reminds the reader that considerations as yet unforeseen may well dictate changes in this initial plan. The language of the design and methods discussion is sure, positive, and active, while reserving the right to modify what is currently proposed.

The second theme, introduced above, is that the proposal is *an argument.* Because the proposal's primary purpose is to convince the reader that the research is substantive, will contribute to the field, is well conceived, and that the researcher is capable of conducting the research, it should rely on supportive reasoning, marshall evidence sufficient to convince the reader of the points, and carefully argue the logic undergirding the proposal. All this will demonstrate a thorough knowledge of both the topic to be explored and the methods to be used. At times we give guidance and use terminology that should assist in translating qualitative design assumptions to more quantitatively oriented audiences. Finally, in thinking of the proposal as an argument, we often mention *the reader* (of the proposal) to remind the reader (of this book) that a sense of audience is critically important in crafting a solid research proposal.

2 The Substance of the Study

FRAMING THE RESEARCH QUESTION

What is research? What is a research proposal? How do the two relate to each other? For the social scientist or researcher in applied fields, research is a process of trying to gain a better understanding of the complexities of human interactions. Through systematic means, the researcher gathers information about actions and interactions, reflects on their meaning, arrives at and evaluates conclusions, and eventually puts forward an interpretation. Quite unlike its pristine and logical presentation in journal articles—"the reconstructed logic of science" (Kaplan, 1964)— real research is often confusing, messy, intensely frustrating, and fundamentally nonlinear. In critiquing the way journal articles display research as a supremely sequential and objective endeavor, Bargar and Duncan (1982) describe how,

> through such highly standardized reporting practices, scientists inadvertently hide from view the real inner drama of their work, with its intuitive

base, its halting time-line, and its extensive recycling of concepts and perspectives. (p. 2)

The researcher begins with interesting, curious, or anomalous phenomena, which he observes, discovers, or stumbles across. Not unlike the detective work of Sherlock Holmes or the best traditions in investigative reporting, research seeks to explain, describe, or explore the phenomenon chosen for study. The research proposal, then, is a plan for engaging in systematic inquiry to bring about a better understanding of the phenomenon and, increasingly, to change problematic social circumstances. As discussed in Chapter 1, the finished proposal should demonstrate that (1) the research is worth doing; (2) the researcher is competent to conduct the study; and (3) the study is carefully planned and can be executed successfully. But how to begin? This is often the most challenging aspect of developing a solid proposal.

How to Begin

In qualitative inquiry, initial questions for research often come from real-world observations, dilemmas, and questions and have emerged from the interplay of the researcher's direct experience, tacit theories, and growing scholarly interests. At other times, the topic of interest derives from theoretical traditions and their attendant empirical research. Beginning researchers should examine reviews of literature found in journals specifically committed to publishing extensive review articles (e.g., *Review of Educational Research),* peruse policy-oriented publications to learn about current or emerging issues in their field, and talk with experts for their judgments about crucial issues. They might also reflect on the intersection of their personal and professional interests to ascertain what particular topics or issues capture their imaginations. Figure 2.1 provides a schematic description of the iterative relationship among theory, empirical research, and personal experience. Often called the "wheel of science," it suggests that the research focus and the place to begin can be identified at any point in this complex process. In turn, this focus provides insights for guiding hypotheses, sites, and samples. They iteratively (and sometimes reiteratively) force decisions about researcher role and strategies for data gathering. And thus on goes the research cycle.

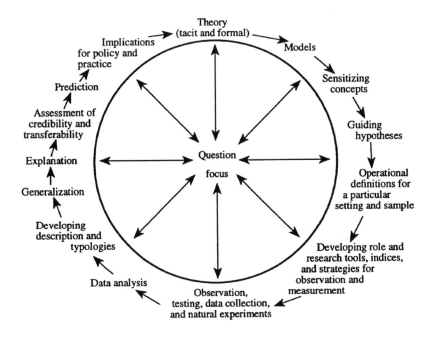

Figure 2.1. A Model of the Research Cycle

Especially in applied fields, such as management, education, and clinical psychology, a strong autobiographical element often drives the scholarly interest. For example, a doctoral student in family counseling psychology studied bereaved mothers because of her own experience with the loss of a teenaged son (Oliver, 1990). A student in social psychology, deeply committed to the protection of the environment, studied environmental attitudes from an adult development theoretical perspective (Greenwald, 1992). A student in organizational development investigated physicians' espoused moral principles of care and justice (as a way of exploring Gilligan's [1982b] theory) in compensation issues because of her deep commitment to ethical practice (Cormier, 1993).

The researcher's challenge is to demonstrate that this personal interest will not bias the study. A sensitive awareness of the methodological literature about the self in conducting inquiry, interpreting data, and constructing the final narrative helps, as does knowledge of the epistemological

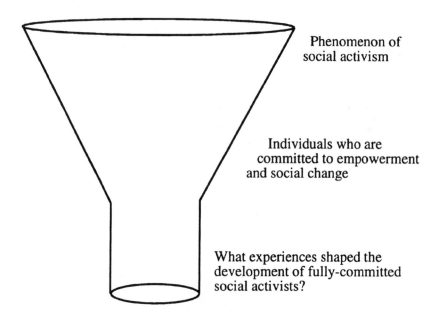

Phenomenon of
social activism

Individuals who are
committed to empowerment
and social change

What experiences shaped the
development of fully-committed
social activists?

Figure 2.2. The Conceptual Funnel

debate about what constitutes knowledge and knowledge claims, especially the critique of power and dominance in traditional research (see the discussion in Chapter 1 about critical ethnography and feminist research). If direct experience stimulates the initial curiosity, moreover, then the researcher needs to link that curiosity to general questions. The large end of the conceptual funnel, if you will, contains the broad questions that the study will explore; the small end, the specific focus for that investigation.

Figure 2.2 provides a depiction of this metaphor (from the work of Benbow, 1994), where the large end represents the general conceptual focus, in this case, the issue of social activism and its role in ameliorating oppressive circumstances. Midway down the funnel, the focus narrows to a concern with *individuals* who have demonstrated and lived an intense commitment to social causes. An alternative choice at this point would have been to focus on social movements as group phenomena, rather than on individuals whose lived experiences embody social consciousness. The small end of the conceptual funnel focuses even more closely on a research question (or set of questions) about how life experiences helped shape and develop a lifelong, intensive commitment to social activism.

People develop personal theories (theories-in-use or tacit theories) about events as ways of reducing ambiguity and explaining paradox. When they decide to conduct inquiry, however, they should be guided by more systematic considerations, such as existing theory and empirical research. Tacit theory and formal theory (from a literature review) help to bring the question, the curious phenomenon, or the problematic issue into focus and raise it to a more general level. The potential research moves from a troubling or intriguing real-world observation (e.g., these kids just won't volunteer in class no matter how much it's rewarded!), to personal theory (these kids care more about what other kids think than they do about grades), to formal theory, concepts, and models from literature (students' behavior is a function of the formal classroom expectations as mediated by the informal expectations of the student subculture). These coalesce to frame a focused research question: What are the expectations of the student subculture vis-à-vis class participation?

Evertson and Green's (1985) framework vividly demonstrates this process of conceptualizing and decision making prior to data collection (see Figure 2.3). Their framework shows the interplay of personal observation with a theoretical rationale that leads to focusing the research question and making decisions about where to go, what to look for, and how to ask questions during real-world observations, whether in a classroom, in an urban neighborhood, or in a hospital ward. Although developed for classroom observation, their model serves as a wonderfully transferable guide. It also points to the cyclical nature of research by ending with a description of research to come.

This early conceptualization work is the most difficult and intellectually rigorous of the entire process of proposal writing. It is messy and iterative, as alternative frames (scholarly traditions) are examined for their power to illuminate and sharpen the research focus. Exploring possible designs and methods enters into this initial process. The process also entails loss as the researcher, captivated by a topic, must let go of some promising research questions in order to bound the study and ensure its do-ability.

The role of intuition in this phase of the research process cannot be underestimated. Studies of eminent scientists reveal the central role of creative insight—intuition—in their thought processes (Hoffman, 1972; Libby, 1922; Mooney, 1951). By allowing ideas to incubate, and through

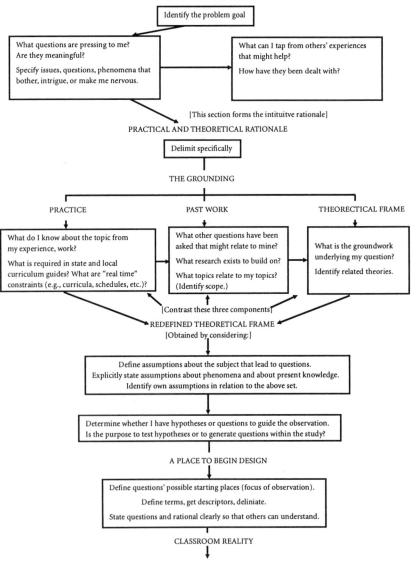

PERSONAL THEORY PHRASE

Identify the problem goal

What questions are pressing to me?
Are they meaningful?

Specify issues, questions, phenomena that
bother, intrigue, or make me nervous.

What can I tap from others' experiences
that might help?

How have they been dealt with?

[This section forms the intituitve rationale]

PRACTICAL AND THEORETICAL RATIONALE

Delimit specifically

THE GROUNDING

PRACTICE   PAST WORK   THEORECTICAL FRAME

What do I know about the topic from
my experience, work?

What is required in state and local
curriculum guides? What are "real time"
constraints (e.g., curricula, schedules, etc.)?

What other questions have been
asked that might relate to mine?

What research exists to build on?

What topics relate to my topics?
(Identify scope.)

What is the groundwork
underlying my question?

Identify related theories.

[Contrast these three components]

REDEFINED THEORETICAL FRAME
[Obtained by considering:]

Define assumptions about the subject that lead to questions.
Explicitly state assumptions about phenomena and about present knowledge.
Identify own assumptions in relation to the above set.

Determine whether I have hypotheses or questions to guide the observation.
Is the purpose to test hypotheses or to generate questions within the study?

A PLACE TO BEGIN DESIGN

Define questions' possible starting places (focus of observation).

Define terms, get descriptors, deliniate.

State questions and rational clearly so that others can understand.

CLASSROOM REALITY

Figure 2.3. A Framework to Guide Decision Making in Observation
SOURCE: From Evertson, C. M., & Green, J. L., "Observation as Inquiry and Method." Reprinted with permission of Macmillan Publishing Company from *Handbook of Research on Teaching* (3rd. ed., pp. 162-213). Merlin C. Wittrock, Editor. Copyright © 1986 by the American Educational Research Association.

maintaining a respect for the mind's capacity for reorganization and reconstruction, the researcher finds that richer research questions evolve. This

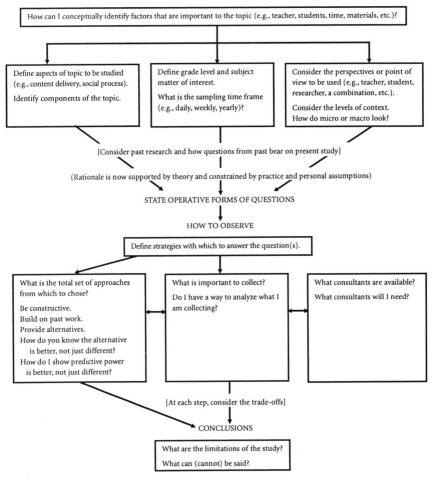

How can I conceptually identify factors that are important to the topic (e.g., teacher, students, time, materials, etc.)?

Define aspects of topic to be studied (e.g., content delivery, social process).

Identify components of the topic.

Define grade level and subject matter of interest.

What is the sampling time frame (e.g., daily, weekly, yearly)?

Consider the perspectives or point of view to be used (e.g., teacher, student, researcher, a combination, etc.).

Consider the levels of context.
How do micro or macro look?

[Consider past research and how questions from past bear on present study]

(Rationale is now supported by theory and constrained by practice and personal assumptions)

STATE OPERATIVE FORMS OF QUESTIONS

HOW TO OBSERVE

Define strategies with which to answer the question(s).

What is the total set of approaches from which to chose?

Be constructive.
Build on past work.
Provide alternatives.
How do you know the alternative is better, not just different?
How do I show predictive power is better, not just different?

What is important to collect?

Do I have a way to analyze what I am collecting?

What consultants are available?

What consultants will I need?

[At each step, consider the trade-offs]

CONCLUSIONS

What are the limitations of the study?
What can (cannot) be said?

DEFINE THE NEXT STUDY TO BE DONE AFTER COMPLETION OF PRESENT STUDY

Figure 2.3. Continued

observation is not intended to devalue the analytic process, but instead to give the creative act its proper due. Again quoting Bargar and Duncan (1982), research is a process:

> that religiously uses logical analysis as a critical tool in the *refinement* of ideas, but which often begins at a very different place, where imagery,

metaphor and analogy, "intuitive hunches," kinesthetic feeling states, and even dreams and dream-like states are prepotent. (p. 3, emphasis in original)

These initial insights and the recycling of concepts begin the process of bounding and framing the research by defining the larger theoretical, policy, or social problem that the study will address; by establishing the study's parameters (what it is and what it is *not);* and by developing a conceptual framework that will ground the study in ongoing research traditions.

Research proposals vary in format but generally include the following three sections: (1) the introduction, which includes an overview of the proposal, a statement of the problem and significance, the focus of the inquiry and research questions, and the limitations of the study; (2) the review of related literature; and (3) the research design and research methods. In all research, these sections are interrelated, each one building on the others. In qualitative inquiry, the proposal should reserve some flexibility in research questions and design because these are likely to change during the research process. The next section provides some strategies for building a clear conceptual framework while retaining the flexibility to allow the unanticipated to emerge.

Introduction to the Study: Problem and Significance, Focus and Research Questions, and Limitations of the Study

The purposes of this section of the proposal are: (1) to describe the substantive focus of the research; (2) to frame it as a larger theoretical, policy, or practical problem and thereby develop its significance; (3) to pose initial research questions; (4) to forecast the literature to be discussed in the second section; and (5) to discuss the limitations of the study. The proposal writer should organize the information so that a reader can clearly ascertain the essence of the research study. This section, along with the review of related literature, forms the conceptual framework of the study and tells the reader the study's substantive focus and purpose. The design section then describes how the study will be conducted and displays the writer's ability to conduct the study.

Although separated into discrete sections through convention, the narrative of the first two sections is derived from a thorough familiarity with literature on relevant theory, empirical studies, and informed essays by knowledgeable experts. A careful reading of related literature serves two purposes. First, it establishes evidence for the significance of the study for practice and policy, and as a contribution to knowledge. Second, it defines and delimits the important intellectual traditions that guide the study, thereby developing a conceptual framework and defining an important and viable research question.

Because of the interrelatedness of the sections and because writing is a developmental, messy task, the writer may find it necessary to rewrite the research questions or problem statement after discussing the literature or to refocus the significance after the research design is developed. Recall Bargar and Duncan's (1982) description of "extensive recycling of concepts and perspectives" (p. 2). Our advice is that the writer be sensitive to the need for change and flexibility and not rush to closure too soon. Sound ideas for research may come in a moment of inspiration, but the hard work comes next as the idea, the intellectual traditions that surround the idea, and the methods for exploring it are developed, refined, and polished.

Introduction

The introductory section of the proposal does just that: It introduces the reader to the problem and significance, research questions, and design of the study. This section should be crisply written, engage the reader's interest, and forecast the sections to follow. First, the problem that the study will address is introduced, linking this to practice, policy, and theory, and forecasting the study's significance. Next, the broad areas of theory and related research to be discussed in the literature review are outlined. Then the design of the study is sketched where the particular approach, major data collection techniques, and unique features of the design are noted. Finally, the introduction provides a transition to a more detailed discussion of the problem, the study's significance, and the research questions.

Defining the Problem and Developing Significance

Convincing the reader that the study is significant and should be conducted entails building an argument that links the research to larger, important theoretical problems, social policy issues, or concerns of practice. The challenge here is to situate the study as addressing a particular, important problem: Defining the problem shapes the study's significance. For instance, a clinical psychologist identifies a theoretical gap in the literature about isolation and defines the problem for an ethnography of long-distance truck drivers as addressing this theoretical problem. The study may be relatively unconcerned with policy or practice; its contributions to theory are preordinate. On the other hand, a feminist sociologist frames a study of discriminatory thinking among business executives as addressing the policy and practice problems of persistent sexism in the workplace. Here, theoretical problems are less significant. The researcher develops the significance of the study through a definition of the problem to be addressed. (Recall the discussion of explicitly ideological research in Chapter 1. For further discussion of these issues, see Smith, 1988.)

A study may well have significance for all three domains, but it is unlikely to contribute equally to all three; the statement of the problem should thus emphasize one particular domain. For example, a study of the integration of children with disabilities into the regular classroom could be significant for both policy and practice. Framing the study as a policy study requires that the problem be situated in national and state education policy on special education. Alternatively, framing the study as most significant for practice would necessitate a problem definition focused on restructuring schools to be more inclusive or on classroom practice to support more diverse students in the regular classroom. Either frame is legitimate and defensible; the researcher's challenge is to identify where the study will contribute the most. This, in turn, has implications for the literature review and the design of the study.

Significance for Theory. The discussion of the study's significance for theory is often an intellectual odyssey for the researcher that is more fully developed in the review of related literature. At this point in the proposal, the researcher should outline the project's contribution to fundamental knowledge by describing how the study fits into theoretical traditions in the social sciences or applied fields in ways that will be new, insightful, or creative. The significance statement should show how the study will contribute to research traditions or foundational literatures in new ways.

Often the proposal identifies gaps in the literature to which the study will contribute. If the research is in an area where theory is well developed, then the study may be a significant test or expansion of the theory. The researcher may use concepts developed by previous researchers and formulate questions

of the underlying assumptions, how the researcher sees the world, and how he sees the research questions fitting in. As the researcher explores theoretical literature, however, he should identify and state those assumptions in a framework of theory. This framework could be child development theory, organizational theory, learning theory, adult socialization theory, or whatever body of theory is appropriate. This section of the literature review provides the framework of the research and identifies the area of knowledge that the study is intended to expand.

The next portion of the review of literature should, quite literally, review and critique previous research that relates to the general question selected. This critical review should lead to a more precise problem statement or refined questions because it demonstrates the specific area that has not yet been adequately explored, or it shows that a different design would be more appropriate. If a major aspect of the significance of the study arises from a reconceptualization of the topic, this is where that should be developed fully. Cooper (1988) provides a discussion of the focus, goal, perspective, coverage, organization, and audience for a literature review. An extended example of the integration and dovetailing of the significance and the review sections of the proposal is described in Vignette 3. Look for the ways the literature review led Marshall (1979, 1981, 1985c) to find new ways to pursue the research questions.

Vignette 3

Significance

When Marshall (1979, 1981, 1985c) was researching the general problem of women's unequal representation in school administration careers, she did not follow the pattern of previous researchers. Many researchers before her had conducted surveys to identify the attributes, the positions, and the percentages of women in school administration. A few researchers had interviewed male and female administrators to identify patterns of discrimination.

In a significant departure from this tradition, Marshall reconceptualized the problem. She looked at it as a problem in the area of adult socialization and looked to career socialization theory. From a review of this body of theory and related empirical research on the school administrative career, including recruitment, training, and selection processes, and on women in jobs and careers, Marshall framed a new question. She asked, "What is the career socialization process for women in school administration? What is the process through which women make career decisions, acquire training and supports, overcome obstacles, and move up in the hierarchy?"

Marshall already knew from previous research that there was discrimination and that women administrators were different from other women. With a background knowledge of organizational theory emphasizing the influence of organizational norms and the power of informal processes, she created a new research question and a different research design. The literature review, therefore, determined the relevant concepts (i.e., norms, informal training) and the tentative guiding hypotheses. The need to identify how this research would be different from previous research focused this literature review. And from this review came the theoretical framework, key concepts, findings from previous research that would guide the new research, and a major aspect of the study's significance. The flow from theory to concepts to tentative hypotheses, moreover, helped focus the research questions.

Once the overall question was identified, the choice of qualitative methods was logical because the question required the exploration of a process not yet identified and not yet encompassed in theory. The research had to build in openness to the unexpected, to new findings, and it had to retain a flexible design that fostered the exploration of nuances of meaning in a complex, tacit process.

This reconceptualization came from asking the significance question: Who cares about this research? The question encouraged a review of previous research that demonstrated how other research had already answered many questions. It showed that women were as competent as men in school administration. But a critical review of this literature argued that this previous research had asked different questions. Marshall could assert that her study would be significant because it would focus on describing a process about which previous research had only guessed. The new research would add to theory by exploring career socialization of women in a profession generally dominated by men. It would also identify the relevant social, psychological, and organizational variables that are part of women's career socialization. This established the significance of the research by showing how it would add to knowledge.

The literature review also established the significance of the research for practice and policy with an overview of the issues of affirmative action and equity concerns. Thus the research question, literature review, and research design were all tied in with the significance question. Responding to this question demanded a demonstration that this was an area of knowledge and practice that needed exploration. To ensure exploration, qualitative methods were the most appropriate for the conduct of the study.

As can be seen, the literature review can identify established knowledge and, more important, can develop significance, new questions, and often turn old questions around. This "initiating" function (Rossman & Wilson, 1994) of the literature review can be quite creative. This review, moreover, provides the intellectual "glue" for the entire proposal, demonstrating the sections' conceptual relatedness. The researcher cannot write about the study's significance without knowledge of the literature. Similarly, she cannot describe the design without the general problem statement. The dissertation proposal is divided into sections because of tradition and convention; there is no magic to these divisions. To organize complex topics and to address the three critical questions posed at the beginning, however, the structure provided here is recommended. Another vignette illustrates how the conceptualization of a study can be creative and exciting, as the researcher forges links among historically disparate literatures.

Vignette 4

Creative Review

When research questions explore new territory, previous literature and theory may be inadequate for constructing frameworks for the study. A case in point is that of Christman (1987), a graduate student in educational administration who searched the literature for a way to frame her study of women returning to graduate school.

Christman's forays into the literature on returning women students and her interaction with faculty and colleagues suggested a number of relevant and provocative questions for her research. Previous studies identified and described demographics about returning women and evaluated the effectiveness of support programs for these women. Many of these studies employed survey or quasi-experimental research designs focused on outcomes and/or products. It became clear that previous research failed to conceptualize the problem in terms of process. With an emphasis on experience, the meaning of experience, and development over time, a process conceptualization placed the study in the theoretical domains of adult socialization. The goal of the research then became the description and analysis of contexts, interactions, and processes.

Continuing to examine the graduate school experience of returning women students, Christman believed that placement of this experience within the context of psychosocial development would illuminate its meaning for the participant. Indeed, recent research had suggested a direct link between a woman's life stage and her understanding of her educational experience.

A curiosity about women's management of two domains—expressive/relational/domestic and instrumental/public/work—during the child-rearing years provided Christman with another set of questions about the returning women students' experience. Piqued originally by Friedan's (1981) *The Second Stage,* this curiosity was then reinforced by the work of a growing number of social scientists who have called for research that explores the dynamic interaction of these domains (Giele, 1982; Kanter, 1977; Piotrkowski, 1979; Smelser & Erikson, 1980). Such interaction is complex. In some instances the two domains may merge so completely as to render the distinction between the two largely artificial. At the same time, the construct of overlapping domains seemed useful in conceptualizing the study.

Christman quoted Kanter (1977) to describe the interplay among field data, literature, and the researcher's introspection:

The other important base for this study should not be neglected. This was, of course, an extensive review of the sociological, social psychological, psychological, and organizational behavior literatures. I considered this a part of the study critical to its success. I worked back and forth between the literature and the field. I formulated hypotheses and questions from the literature, and I could test the generalizability of my field observations through the literature review.

With C. Wright Mills I believe that reading can also be a valid form of research. (p. 298)

That no single strand of theoretical or empirical literature encompassed the entirety of her research questions was clear from the outset. Literature on returning women graduate students focused on the evaluation of programs designed to overcome obstacles. Literature acknowledging the interface of love and work was just emerging. With this emergence came the overthrow of the functionalists' assumptions that the institutions of family and workplace were divided into emotional and geographical units that were specialized in their separate activities, without mutual interference (Pleck, 1976, p. 179).

The relatively recent attention given to the developmental nature of adulthood by social psychology focused primarily on the life stages of men. Critiques by Gilligan (1982a, 1982b) and Chodorow (1978) indicated that the values and dreams of women involved in the study differed from those of men. Socialization theory pointed to role acquisition, the development of commitment to a profession, and the impact of formal and informal structures in graduate school that affect those being socialized in different ways.

Although Christman's literature review did not precisely set her research question within a particular framework, it did expose missing areas and the questions raised by existing literature. It also underscored her work as research into unexplored territory that promised to identify new ways of connecting previous knowledge to new grounded theory.

Vignette 4 shows a creative blending of several strands of literature for framing the research. The integration of literatures helped shape a research focus that was theoretical in interest yet could help inform policy at the organizational level. Broad reading and knowledge of sociological role theory, adult development, organizational structures and processes, and feminist theory provided a rich background for this creative synthesis. Rather than narrowly constructing the study to focus on only one of the above topics, the author searched widely for illuminating constructs from other disciplines. Such work, though at times tedious, confusing, and ambiguous, enhances the research to follow and demonstrates that the researcher has engaged in significant intellectual work already.

Another example of integrative literature reviews comes from a study conducted by Rossman, Corbett, and Firestone (1988). Framed as a study of high school cultures undergoing change, the conceptual framework and research design for the study had to address fundamental definitional questions about change, culture, and the interaction of the two. They then had to argue that these notions applied to schools. Specifically, the researchers were challenged to blend distinctive writings on organizational culture (derived from social anthropology and applied in organizational behavior studies), change in social systems (found in sociology, social psychology, and again organizational behavior), and recent research depicting and analyzing the complex processes of what was then called school improvement (today we would call this restructuring). Vignette 5 describes this framework development.

Vignette 5

Using Concepts

As part of an ongoing interest in school improvement and school change, the Applied Research Group at Research for Better Schools became interested in exploring the notion of culture as a lens for viewing school change, improvement initiatives, and mandates for reform. This interest arose because the researchers believed that a significant portion of the effective schools research expressed or implied that school culture was a significant aspect of effectiveness. More important than any one particular finding, Rossman, Corbett, and Firestone (1984) argued, was the way those elements were melded together to create a school culture that supported and encouraged learning and respect for one another.

These ideas were developed into a conceptual framework and research design (Rossman, 1985) that guided the study. The conceptual framework explored literatures from four traditions: anthropology, sociology, organization theory, and education. The first three were drawn on to build the definition of culture that guided the research, emphasizing the descriptive and prescriptive aspects of culture. Next, the researchers turned to the literatures on cultural change and transformation, some of which had been applied to the study of organizations, and the literature on educational change and innovation.

These traditions were used to develop the idea that change in school culture could be conceptualized as evolutionary, additive, or transformative. Further examination of the literature on educational innovation and implementation helped refine this into the idea that change initiatives (broadly construed) could affect school culture. This search identified places where the concept of culture was relied on either directly or implicitly.

Finally, a search through the literature on successful schools and other types of organizations generated five domains, or large categories of meaning, that might well be present in schools in the process of fundamental changes in their meaning structures. These domains encompassed two basic sets of questions about organizations and organizing. First, how did those who participated in this organization relate to one another in the workplace? What were the norms governing how they interacted? The two domains identified here were *collegiality* and *community*.

The second set of questions captured how participants defined the nature of the work. How were goals and expectations for others defined? Was there a belief in taking risks that was supported by others? And what constituted knowledge among those actors? To what authorities were claims made? Three domains were described to capture this set of questions: *goals and expectations, action orientation or risk taking,* and *knowledge base.* Together these five domains fostered a creative use of literature outside the field of education and helped frame data collection for the research project.

The literature review serves many purposes for the research. It supports the importance of the study's focus and may serve to validate the eventual findings in a narrowly descriptive study. It also guides the development of explanations during data collection and analysis in studies that seek to explain, evaluate, and suggest linkages among events. In grounded theory development, the literature review provides theoretical constructs, categories, and their properties that can be used to organize the data and discover new connections between theory and real-world phenomena.

The sections of the proposal discussed thus far—introduction, problem statement and significance, focus of the study and general research questions, and literature review—stand together as the conceptual body of the proposal. Here the major (and minor) ideas for the proposal are developed, their intellectual roots are displayed and critiqued, and the writings and studies of other researchers are presented and critiqued. All of this endeavor is intended to tell the reader what the research is about (its subject), who ought to care about it (its significance), and what others have described and concluded about the subject (its intellectual roots). All three purposes are interwoven into these sections of the proposal.

The final major section—research design and methods—must flow conceptually and logically from all that has gone before. Here the researcher makes a case, based on the conceptual portion of the proposal, for the particular methods, sample, data analysis techniques, and reporting format chosen for the study. Thus the section on design and methods should build a rationale for decisions about the study's overall design and specific data collection methods. Here the researcher should develop a case for the selection of qualitative methods.

We recommend most strongly that the researcher not decide to do a qualitative study and then search for a research problem. The methods should be linked epistemologically with the problem and the research questions. In fact, novice researchers sometimes pose questions that demand quantitative responses and then find themselves in a quandary because they believed they were developing a proposal for qualitative work! Other times they suppose that quantitative research will be easier to conduct. Researchers should design the study according to the research questions they seek to answer. This suggests, of course, that there are many questions not appropriate to pursue through qualitative methods.

Although there are parallels, qualitative and more traditional quantitative proposals differ. In the development of a qualitative proposal, the researcher first orients the proposal reader to the general problem or questions to be explored. This will not be a statement of specific research questions, propositions to be tested, or hypotheses to be examined. A qualitative problem statement may be a general discussion of the puzzle, unexplored issue, or group to be studied. It becomes more precise and focused through the literature review that often includes several bodies of literature because, in exploratory studies, it is hard to predict which literature will be most relevant and encompassing.

In some cases the literature review yields cogent and useful definitions, constructs, concepts, and even data collection strategies. These may fruitfully result in a set of guiding hypotheses. Using such a phrase—*guiding hypothesis*—may assist readers accustomed to more traditional proposals.

It is essential, however, that the researcher explain that guiding hypotheses are merely tools used to generate questions and to search for patterns, and may be discarded when the researcher gets into the field and finds other exciting patterns of phenomena. This approach retains the flexibility needed to allow the precise focus of the research to evolve during the research process itself. By avoiding precise hypotheses, the researcher retains her right to explore and *generate* hypotheses in the general area of the problem statement. The guiding hypotheses illustrate for the reader some possible directions the researcher may follow. The researcher, however, is still free to discover and pursue other patterns.

We do not intend to suggest that proposal development proceeds in a linear fashion. As noted in Chapter 1, conceptualizing a study and developing a design that is clear, flexible, and manageable is iterative, messy, and just plain hard work. As the researcher plays with concepts and theoretical frames for the study, she often entertains alternative designs, assessing them for their power to address the emerging questions. Considering an ethnography, a case study, or an in-depth interview study as the overall design will in turn reshape the research questions. And so the process continues as the conceptual framework and specific design features become more and more elegantly related. The challenge is to build the logical connections between the problem, the questions, and the design and methods, to which we now turn.

3

How to Conduct the Study

DESIGNING THE RESEARCH

T he section of the research proposal devoted to a description of the design and methods serves three major purposes. First, it presents a plan for the conduct of the study. Second, it demonstrates to the reader that the researcher is capable of conducting the study. And third, it should preserve the design flexibility that is a hallmark of qualitative methods. This latter purpose is often the most challenging.

There are typically eight major topics addressed in this section: the overall approach and rationale; site and sample selection; the researcher's role; data collection methods; data management; data analysis strategy; trustworthiness features; and a management plan or time line. Woven into these topics are the twin challenges described above: the need to present a clear, doable plan balanced by the necessity of maintaining some flexibility in the implementation of that plan. After a discussion of these challenges, the first three topics are discussed. The next two chapters then discuss data collection methods (Chapter 4) and strategies for managing and analyzing qualitative data (Chapter 5). Because managing the entire research process (using a management plan and time line) and trustworthiness considerations require extended discussion, they are presented in Chapters 6 and 7, respectively.

Meeting the Challenges

How do researchers maintain the needed flexibility of research design, so that the research can "unfold, cascade, roll, and emerge" (Lincoln & Guba, 1985, p. 210), and yet present a plan that is logical, concise, thorough, and meets the criterion of do-ability? The research design section should demonstrate to the reader that the overall plan is sound, and that the researcher is competent to undertake the research, capable of employing the methods arrayed, and sufficiently interested to sustain the effort necessary for the successful completion of the study.

The researcher should demonstrate to the reader that she reserves the right to design the research *as it evolves:* Building flexibility into the design is crucial. The researcher does this by (1) demonstrating the appropriateness and the logic of qualitative methods for the particular research question; and (2) devising a research plan that includes many of the elements of traditional plans but reserves the right to modify and change that initial plan during data collection. This section of the qualitative proposal should include a statement of the rationale and logic of qualitative methods that undergirds the choice of an overall approach, as well as the sections delineating various elements of the design mentioned above.

The Overall Strategy and a Rationale

Although general acceptance of qualitative inquiry is currently widespread, particularly in education, at times it is necessary to provide a rationale for research grounded in the assumptions of the qualitative or interpretive paradigm. The most compelling argument is to stress the unique strengths of this paradigm for research that is exploratory or descriptive, that assumes the value of context and setting, and that searches for a deeper understanding of the participants' lived experiences of the phenomenon. One critical assumption follows Thomas's (1949) proposition that, in the study of human experience, it is essential to know how people define their situations: "If men [sic] define situations as real, they are real in their consequences" (p. 301). Explicating the logical and compelling connections—the epistemological integrity—between the research questions, the design, and the methods is often quite convincing.

Overall Strategy

In determining the soundest research strategy, Yin (1984) proposes three questions. First, what is the form of the research question—is it exploratory? Does it seek to describe the incidence or distribution of some phenomenon or does it try to explain some social phenomenon? Second, does the research require control over behavior, or does it seek to describe naturally occurring events? And third, is the phenomenon under study contemporary or historical?

Answers to these questions suggest the choice of one research strategy over another. Yin (1984) identifies five distinct strategies: experiments, surveys, archival analyses, histories, and case studies (pp. 13-20). To these we would add more explicitly qualitative strategies such as field studies, ethnographies (a special case of field studies), and in-depth interview studies. Table 3.1 provides the researcher with a framework for deciding on the most adequate and efficient research strategy. Although Yin (1984) would assert that a strategy does not ipso facto determine particular data collection methods, we have found that qualitative methods often define a particular strategy. If the explicitly qualitative strategies mentioned above are added to Yin's list, then a typology is generated that has both method-specific and method-open choices. Addressing the categories shown in Table 3.1 will help the researcher make decisions about the overall strategy and the most useful data collection methods.

Though the selection of a research strategy does not *necessarily* dictate the use of qualitative data collection methods (as with histories or case studies, for example), when discussing the strategy, the writer should mention the use of qualitative methods and discuss why that decision was made. The strategy is a road map, an overall plan for undertaking a systematic exploration of the phenomenon of interest; the methods are the specific tools for conducting that exploration. A history, for example, could rely on an array of methods ranging from in-depth interviewing to retrieval of census data. A case study could similarly use several methods to elicit

Table 3.1   Matching Research Questions With Strategy

Purpose of the Study	Research Question	Research Strategy	Examples of Data Collection Techniques
EXPLORATORY to investigate little-understood phenomena to identify/discover important variables to generate hypotheses for further research	What is happening in this social program? What are the salient themes, patterns, categories in participants' meaning structures? How are these patterns linked with one another?	case study field study	participant observation in-depth interviewing elite interviewing
EXPLANATORY to explain the forces causing the phen-omenon in question to identify plausible causal networks shaping the phenomenon	What events, beliefs, attitudes, policies are shaping this phenomenon? How do these forces interact to result in the phenomenon?	multisite case study history field study ethnography	participant observation in-depth interviewing survey questionnaire document analysis
DESCRIPTIVE to document the phenomenon of interest	What are the salient behaviors, events, beliefs, attitudes, structures, processes occurring in this phenomenon?	field study case study ethnography	participant observation in-depth interviewing document analysis unobtrusive measures survey questionnaire
PREDICTIVE to predict the outcomes of the phenomenon to forecast the events and behaviors resulting from the phenomenon	What will occur as a result of this phenomenon? Who will be affected? In what ways?	experiment quasi-experiment	survey questionnaire (large sample) kinesics/proxemics content analysis

the desired information. Some methods are usually associated with specific strategies, but rather than dictating whether qualitative or quantitative data will be gathered, the overall approach frames the study by placing bounda-ries around it, identifying the level of analytic interest (person, group, program, organization, interorganization), and specifying whether interest is in the past or in the present. The research strategy thus reflects a series of major decisions made by the researcher in an attempt to ascertain the best approach to the research questions posed in the conceptual portion of the proposal.

In developing the overall approach to the study—its strategy—Zelditch (1962) has proposed that qualitative research should be judged on two criteria. The first is *informational adequacy*. Does the research design maximize the possibilities that the researcher will be able to respond to the questions thoroughly and thoughtfully? Will the strategy elicit the sought-after information? The second criterion is *efficiency*. Does the plan allow adequate data to be collected at the least cost in terms of time, access, and cost to participants?

To these we would add *ethical considerations* as a critical criterion against which to judge research strategies. Will the proposed strategy violate the participants' privacy or unduly disrupt their everyday worlds? Are they putting themselves in danger or at risk by participating in the study? Will the study violate their human rights in some way?

The range of possible qualitative strategies is small; choice depends on the focus for the research and on the desired time frame for the study. Examples of qualitative strategies include case studies, life histories, in-depth interview studies, and field studies. Various typologies of qualitative strategies often include ethnographies, which are special cases of field studies, deriving from cultural anthropology and relying on a specific set of constructs.

If the research is focused on the development and evaluation of a college's distinctive ethos, as was Burton Clark's (1970), then selecting the case study strategy, using historical methods, is a sound choice. If the research focus is on complex interactions between an adult with cognitive challenges and her social world, then a life history would be the most appropriate research strategy. The choice is shaped by the general research questions and the theoretical framework provided by the literature review.

To further buttress the rationale for qualitative inquiry and the overall strategy, discussion of a pilot study can be quite important. Description and assessment of a qualitative pilot study supports the researcher's claim that she is capable of conducting the proposed study. Even without a pilot study, the researcher can illustrate the ability to manage qualitative research by describing initial observations or interviews. These experiences usually reveal fascinating questions and intriguing patterns. A description of initial observations demonstrates not only the ability to manage this research, but also the strengths of qualitative methods for generating enticing research questions. Inclusion of a description of a pilot study or initial observations thus often strengthens the proposal.

In addition to developing a strong, supported rationale for the qualitative approach, this section of the proposal should preserve the right to modify aspects of the research design as the research proceeds. Early investigations into the phenomenon can also demonstrate the benefits of maintaining some flexibility. Geer's (1969) description of "first days in the field" illustrates this. She describes the qualitative researcher's immersion in the setting, beginning with the concepts, processes, or variables that have been identified in previous research, guided by the theoretical framework and derived hypotheses. These help the researcher determine what situations to observe, whom to interview, and what to ask. The researcher should establish the need and right to determine the precise focus of the research *after* these first days in the field, after that experience begins to clarify the relevant themes and patterns.

The researcher should develop a justification for the choice of a strategy and qualitative methods. He should show how and why the research question will be best addressed in a natural setting, using this exploratory approach. Here, the strengths of qualitative studies should be emphasized by expanding on the value of qualitative studies for the following types of research (Marshall, 1985a, 1987):

- research that delves in depth into complexities and processes
- research on little-known phenomena or innovative systems
- research that seeks to explore where and why policy and local knowledge and practice are at odds
- research on informal and unstructured linkages and processes in organizations
- research on real, as opposed to stated, organizational goals
- research that cannot be done experimentally for practical or ethical reasons
- research for which relevant variables have yet to be identified

Further support is found in the assertions of Wilson (1977) about the strengths of qualitative methods. He argues that human behavior is significantly influenced by the setting in which it occurs, thus one must study that behavior in situations. The physical setting—for example, schedules, space, pay, and rewards—and the internalized notions of norms, traditions, roles, and values are crucial contextual variables. Research should be conducted in the setting where all the contextual variables are operating. Furthermore, he argues that one cannot understand human behavior without understanding the framework within which participants interpret their thoughts, feelings, and actions; researchers, therefore, need to understand those frameworks. In fact, the "objective" scientist, by coding and standardizing, may destroy valuable data while imposing her world on the subjects. Finally, in further critiquing experimental models, Wilson notes that past researchers have not been able to derive meaning and useful findings from experimental research, and that the research techniques themselves, in experimental research, have affected the findings. The lab, the questionnaire, and so on, have become artifacts. Subjects are either suspicious and wary, or they are aware of what the researchers want and try to please them.

In short, the strengths of qualitative studies should be demonstrated for research that is exploratory or descriptive and that stresses the importance of context, setting, and the participants' frames of reference. A well-reasoned and convincing rationale for qualitative methods is presented in Vignette 6.

In a proposal for a long-term study of the local implementation of state school improvement programs, Rossman, Wilson, and Corbett (1985) developed a concise but strong rationale for the use of qualitative methods. The rationale was firmly grounded in the conceptual framework proposed for the study and showed how the selection of methods should flow from the research questions. (Vignette 6 is directly excerpted from Rossman et al., 1985, pp. 1-2, 19-20.)

Vignette 6

Rationale for Qualitative Research: A Cultural Perspective on the Local Implementation of State School Improvement Programs

"We simply cannot understand organizational phenomena without considering culture both as a cause and as a way of explaining such phenomena" (Schein, 1985, p. 311).

The significance of organizational culture as a way of understanding, describing, and explaining complex social phenomena has been increasingly acknowledged by students of organizations, consultants to organizations, and those of us who spend most of our workday lives within organizations. Moreover, students of educational organizations have found the concept of culture elusive but powerful in understanding the complexities of schools and schooling.

The research proposed here would undertake an in-depth, long-term exploration of how the cultures of twelve schools are modified and transformed as a result of state-initiated improvement programs. Underlying the proposed research is the guiding assumption that although such programs do not typically attend to the culture of schools, features of these programs can profoundly alter core values and beliefs. Cultural transformation, then, may be one of the unintended by-products of state-initiated programs. Since cultural norms and values are being increasingly recognized as crucial for understanding organizational change and effectiveness (see, e.g., Schein, 1985), one benefit of this study will be to describe those unintended but critical effects.

The research approach is a longitudinal, multi-site case study of improvement programs in twelve schools in four states. Sites will be selected that provide the greatest potential for revealing cultural transformation in response to a state-initiated improvement program. Data collection will consist of structured and unstructured interviewing and observation in the twelve schools. Periodic site visits will allow us to track change processes over time and to generate detailed knowledge of each school.

Research Approach

A cultural perspective for a study of local reactions to state-initiated school improvement programs suggests particular methods that are congruent with the perspective's assumptions. First, a cultural perspective requires an in-depth look into the improvement process. To fully understand the impact of the improvement on the school culture a set of 12 schools is proposed for case study. A researcher will spend at least 25 days at each site to gain an in-depth understanding of the cultural aspects of the improvement process. This will provide sufficient time to get beneath the surface of the school's culture, to observe behavior, and to become familiar with key actors. It will also allow time to explore the development, maintenance, and alteration of the school's culture over time.

Second, because it is so difficult to generalize from single cases (Kennedy, 1979), the research will focus on cross-site analyses that identify major patterns (Herriott & Firestone, 1983). This approach recognizes both the need to inform policy-makers and the importance of local variation (Corbett, Dawson, & Firestone, 1984) that cannot be explored unless the cases are compared. Thus, while preserving holistic data from specific sites, it is important to conduct more general, comparative analyses concerning implementation of school improvement efforts at the local level.

Finally, the research will rely on interviews as the primary method of data collection. The purpose of the interviews will be to have local practitioners reflect on recent behavior. In addition, it will allow the researchers to discuss in detail cultural changes. With schools that are currently undergoing these mandated improvement efforts, any changes will be fresh in people's minds and, thus, the reconstruction of events will be possible. Interviews will allow us to trace the development of improvement efforts as perceived by the local staff. We will be particularly interested in their accounts of events, their responses [to] and interpretations of those events, and how they have negotiated with the sources of changes and among themselves to create an emergent improvement orientation. In-depth interviews with multiple informants at each site will also allow us to triangulate findings across sources and test issues of reliability and validity.

Vignette 6 offers an illustration of researchers effectively arguing for a cultural perspective and in-depth data collection. The proposal contained detailed information about data collection that would be in sufficient depth to foster "thick description" of the social systems undergoing substantial change. This level of detail provides answers to funding agencies' questions and concerns, as well as guiding the intensive fieldwork planned for the project.

One purpose of the research design section is to demonstrate that the researcher is capable of conducting qualitative research. Taking courses in qualitative methodology or reading about it will provide a wealth of examples to draw on. The use of quotes and citations of other researchers' work demonstrates a knowledge of the ongoing methodological discourse about qualitative inquiry. An increasing number of researchers have provided descriptions of the rationale and evolving research design: Campbell, in *The Girls in the Gang* (1984); Lesko, in *Symbolizing Society* (1988); Metz, in *Classrooms and Corridors* (1978); and Valli, in *Becoming Clerical Workers* (1986). Classical discussions are found in Olesen and Whittaker, *The Silent Dialogue* (1967b); Smith, *Anatomy of an Educational Innovation* (1971); and Whyte, *Street Corner Society* (1955).

Once the overall approach and a supporting rationale have been presented, the proposal outlines the setting or population of interest and plans for more specific sampling of people, places, and events. This outline provides the reader with a sense of the scope of the proposed inquiry and whether the intensity, amount, and variability of the data will encourage full responses to the research questions. In addition, the proposal should address issues of the researcher's role, including entry, reciprocity, and ethics; specific planned data collection techniques; how the data will be recorded and managed; initial strategies for data analysis; design features for ensuring the trustworthiness of the study; and a management plan with a time line for the conduct and final reporting of the study.

The research design section can deal with these issues through the use of plentiful and relevant quotes from the writings of experts. For example, to explain researcher ethics relative to participants, the experience of Krieger (1985) studying a lesbian community is useful and compelling. Similarly, the conceptual framework developed through the literature review can suggest possible categories or themes for data analysis.

Finally, when possible, it is useful to include a hypothesized model or an outline of possible interview questions and observation and coding categories. These can be developed from a pilot study or from the literature review. Such a model or outline will demonstrate that the researcher has an understanding of how to start looking at behaviors when she enters the field and that she has an initial approach to analyzing the data. Table 3.2 presents an example of categories for observation in a qualitative study.

In the research design for *Power Language and Women's Access to Organizational Leadership,* Marshall (1986) took an interdisciplinary approach, using kinesics, proxemics, observation, and interviewing to examine the language and interactions of middle-management men and women. The study proposed a hypothesis, based on sociolinguistic research, that women

Table 3.2   Observations and Coding Categories for *Power Language and
Women's Access to Organizational Leadership*

I.   Verbal
     A.   tone
          1. pitch
          2. loudness
          3. intonation
     B.   duration
          1. length of sentence
          2. conciseness
     C.   content
          1. tag questions
          2. phrases of tentativeness: I believe, I guess, I think
          3. apologies
          4. self-denigration
          5. niceties
          6. humor—dirty jokes/elaborate/quick asides
          7. metaphors—sports
          8. four-letter words
          9. parts of speech: verbs, adjectives, pronouns (royal we)
          10. power language: aggressive, put-downs, patronizing, soft voice for
              dramaturgical purposes, refer to experts
              a. self (years of experience)
              b. outside experts
          11. political and value statements
          12. exhibiting naïveté
     D.   silences
          1. wait time
          2. dramatization
II. Nonverbal
     A.   kinesics
          1. face
              a. eyes
              b. rest of face
          2. hands
          3. stance
          4. idiosyncratic
          5. legs
     B.   proxemics
          1. use of space
              a. moving around room
              b. moving from chair
          2. desk—props
          3. spread of territory
          4. control of decor
     C.   appearance
          1. dress
          2. makeup
          3. hair
          4. accessories

(continued)

Table 3.2   Continued

              a. personal
              b. work-related
        5. facial hair

III. Audience reaction
    A.   distraction
        1. asides
        2. paper shuffling
        3. off-task behavior
        4. humor
        5. leaving group
        6. body position changes
        7. criticize speech
            a. power language asides
            b. ask to speak louder
    B.   engagement and feedback
        1. head nodding
        2. smiling
        3. looking at speaker
        4. eye contact
        5. verbal agreements/critiques
        6. asking questions
            a. on-task
            b. clarification
        7. body positioning
    C.   interruption

IV. Macro (global)
    A.   body positioning of groups
    B.   hand gestures
    C.   indications of agreement
    D.   use of objects
    E.   taking a break
    F.   side comments
    G.   amount of time women/men spoke
    H.   arrangement of people map
    I.   formal/informal leader
    J.   amount of times women/men restructure agenda
    K.   how women and men get recognized to speak
    L.   defying group norms
    M.   structured request for assistance
    N.   courtship behavior
    O.   proportion of meeting time utilized by men and women
    P.   female/male structured commands
    Q.   mirroring body movements

V. Combined verbal and nonverbal
    A.   greetings
        1. touching
        2. verbal salutations
    B.   eye pleading with groups

SOURCE: Marshall (1986, Appendix A).

use less power-and-control language and therefore *appear* to have less leadership potential in settings that value power and control. For the reviewers who were deciding whether or not to fund such a nontraditional project, this outline was reassuring. It was developed from a mock-pilot, in which Marshall and four doctoral students observed videotapes of meetings among middle managers and, using the framework from socio-linguistic literature, focused on key language and interaction variables. Reviewers are generally impressed by such concrete evidence of research direction.

Focusing on the Setting, Population, or Phenomenon

In most cases, one cannot study intensively and in depth all instances, events, or persons. One selects samples. The first and most global decision, choosing the setting, population, or phenomenon of interest, is fundamental to the design of the study and serves as a guide for the researcher. This early, significant decision shapes all subsequent ones and should be described and justified clearly.

Some research is site-specific. For example, research that asks, "By what processes do women's studies programs become incorporated into universities?" must focus on a setting where this takes place. In contrast, research that asks, "By what processes do innovative units become incorporated into educational organizations?" has a choice of many sites and many different substantive programs. Questions such as, "By what processes have Peace Corps volunteers been able to effect long-term health improvements in communities?" can be pursued in many sites throughout the world.

The decision to focus on a specific setting (e.g., the Women's Studies Program at the University of Massachusetts) is a fairly constrained choice; the study is defined by and intimately linked to that place. A choice to study a particular population (faculty in women's studies programs) is somewhat less constrained; the study can be conducted in more places than one. The decision to study a phenomenon (the socialization of new faculty) is even less constrained by either place or population. In these latter instances the researcher determines a sampling strategy that is purposeful and representative.

If the study is of a specific program, organization, place, or region, some detail regarding the setting is crucial for the reader. A rationale should also be provided that outlines why this specific setting is more appropriate than others for the conduct of the study. What is unique? What characteristics of this setting are compelling and unusual? Justify this early and highly significant decision.

The ideal site is where (1) entry is possible; (2) there is a high probability that a rich mix of the processes, people, programs, interactions, and structures of interest are present; (3) the researcher is likely to be able to build trusting relations with the participants in the study; and (4) data quality and credibility of the study are reasonably assured. Although this ideal is seldom attained, the proposal nonetheless describes what makes the selection of this particular site especially sound. A site may be perfect for its representativeness, interest, and the range of examples of the phenomena under study, but if the researcher cannot gain access to the site and to a range of groups and activities within it, the study cannot succeed. Similarly, if the researcher is very uncomfortable or endangered in the site, the study will be hampered.

When the focus of the study is on a particular population, the researcher should present a strategy for sampling that population. For example, in a study of forced terminations of psychotherapy, Kahn's (1992) strategy was to post notices in local communities asking for participants. Much discussion ensued at her proposal hearing about the feasibility of this strategy. Given assurances about previous experiences of soliciting participants through this method, the committee agreed; the strategy was ultimately successful.

In the proposal, the researcher should anticipate questions about the credibility and trustworthiness of the findings; poor sampling decisions may threaten these findings. To justify a sample, one must know the universe and all of its relevant variables—an impossible task. Generally, the best compromise is to include a sample with reasonable variation in the phenomenon, settings, or people under study (Dobbert, 1982). Some sampling issues are described in Vignette 7, which may be helpful for researchers thinking through the sampling and site selection issues in any qualitative study.

Vignette 7

Selecting Sites and Sampling

Issues of sampling can be illustrated with community studies. Although the famous Yankee City study seemed to demand a parallel study of the Deep South, how were researchers to identify a city representative of the Deep South? After selecting several cities that fit the criteria of size and history, Warner (reported by Gardner in Whyte, 1984) met with leaders and established contacts in the communities, eventually selecting Natchez as the site for *Deep South: A Social Anthropological Study of Caste and Class* (Davis, Gardner, & Gardner, 1941).

Negotiations for entry and access to various levels of the "caste system" were aided by the involvement of two wife/husband teams, one black and one white. All four individuals were raised in the South and were familiar with appropriate behavior within the caste system, making it possible for them to observe, interview, and participate in activities, interactions, and sentiments representing all levels of the Natchez community, over a period of 1½ years. They were able to record the overt and covert behavior and verbalization associated with significant social institutions, and to do so across race, sex, and age groups, even in the most intimate cliques. According to Warner and Davis, "The methodological aim was to see every negro-white [sic] relationship from both sides of society, so as to avoid a limited 'white view' or a limited 'negro view' [sic]" (in Thompson, 1939, p. 235).

The reports demonstrated that Natchez, although not exactly like all other Southern communities, was *not atypical*. Setting abstract criteria, checking out sites in advance, and careful planning of entry ensured that (1) the research team could move throughout the community to gather data; and (2) Natchez was not an unrepresentative pocket of the research universe.

Vignette 7 provides an illustration of researchers identifying the site that would maximize comparability and allow access to a wide range of behaviors and perspectives. Clearly, the selection of site and sample are critical decisions. Vignette 8 shows how site selection affects the viability of the whole study.

Vignette 8

Selecting a Site to Maximize Access

An actual town, described anonymously as "Elmtown," was selected by the Committee on Human Development of the University of Chicago as typical of Midwestern communities, and therefore a suitable site for what the committee proposed in preliminary contacts with residents as a study of the "character development" of boys and girls (Hollingshead, 1975). One stimulus for the study was the paucity of research done by sociologists on the subject of adolescent behavior.

The researchers, a husband-and-wife team, made several preparatory visits to the community, establishing contacts with civic leaders and getting the lay of the land while locating housing for the 10 months during which the study would be conducted. The specific focus of the study emerged from the prestudy visits and the first 2 months of the researchers' residence in Elmtown. The larger question—Is the social behavior of an adolescent a function of physiological changes in the maturing individual or of his or her experiences in society?—eventually led to the working hypothesis, "The social behavior of adolescents appears to be related to the positions that their families occupy in the status structure of the community" (Hollingshead, 1975, pp. 6-7).

In order to test the hypothesis, data were gathered by the research team in such a way as to disturb the setting as little as possible. They consulted school records and identified 752 boys and girls who either were enrolled in the local high school or should have been enrolled. Of these, 17 were dropped due either to a refusal to cooperate by religious academy officials (12 girls) or the unavailability of data about families' positions in the social structure (5 boys). Excluded were high school graduates and peers who had left school before graduating. The study group therefore consisted of 735 adolescents representing 535 families. Of these young people, 81% had been born in Elmtown, as had 62% of their parents.

The research team participated as full members of the community. They gained access to parents and institutional functionaries by virtue of their stated interest in adolescent "character development" and by minimizing their curiosity with regard to the community as a whole. This interest brought them invitations to speak before a variety of community organizations, resulting in additional contacts. They spent a considerable amount of time in informal settings with young people as well. They were at the high school before school, at noon, and after school; they attended most school activities, church affairs, Scout meetings, dances, and parties; and they skated, bowled, shot pool, played poker, and generally "hung out" where the youth were known to gather. "The observational technique of being with them as often as possible and not criticizing their activities, carrying tales, or interfering overcame the original suspicion in a few weeks" (Hollingshead, 1975, p. 15).

In Vignette 8, what the researchers did *not* say enabled virtually all of Elmtown to become part of the sample for their study. Their ability to gain access to a range of groups and activities was enhanced by their ability to blend in. Site and sample selection should be planned around practical issues, such as the researcher's comfort, ability to fit into some role during participant observation, and access to a range of subgroups and activities. In some proposals, particularly those for multisite studies conducted with several researchers or for studies of organizations, it is wise to make even finer decisions about sampling. This is discussed next.

Sampling People, Behaviors, Events, and/or Processes

Once the initial decision has been made to focus on a specific site, a population, or a phenomenon, waves of subsequent sampling decisions are made. The proposal describes the plan, as conceived before the research begins, that will guide sample selection, always mindful of the need to retain flexibility. Thus the research questions focus site and sample selection; where they do not, the researcher, at the very least, makes explicit the procedures and criteria for decision making.

Well-developed sampling decisions are crucial for any study's soundness. Making logical judgments and presenting a rationale for these decisions go far in building the overall case for a proposed study. Decisions about sampling people and events develop concurrently with decisions about the specific data collection methods to be used and should be thought through in advance. When faced, for example, with the complexity of studying the meaning women managers attach to computer mediated communications, Alvarez (1993) had to decide what individuals and events would be most salient for her study.

Vignette 9

Focusing on People and Events

The general question guiding Alvarez's (1993) study was in what ways computer-mediated communications, specifically electronic mail, alter human communications within an organizational context. She was interested in the power equalization potential of E-mail

communications among persons of unequal status within the
organization; and in the socioemotional content of messages sent and
received in a medium of reduced social cues.

The sampling strategy began as a search for information-rich cases
(Patton, 1990) in order to study individuals who manifested the
phenomenon intensely. A related concern was to have both men and
women participants in the study, given that the theoretical literature
suggested that there are significant differences between men and women
in ease of computer usage. Once participants had been identified and
agreed to engage in the study with Alvarez, she had to make decisions
about which specific events she wanted to observe or learn more about.
She reasoned that observing the sending or receiving of a message would
yield little; she therefore asked participants to share sets of
"correspondence" with her, as well as participate in two in-depth
interviews. The former request proved quite sensitive, as Alvarez was
asking people to share their personal and professional mail with her. She
reassured them of the confidentiality of the study and also showed them
how to send copies of E-mail directly to her without revealing the direct
recipient of the message. This reassured them sufficiently to result in a
substantial set of messages that could then be content analyzed.

A second vignette, a more elaborate one because of the nature of the
study, is taken from the high school cultures study's plan for sampling
(Rossman et al., 1984). This vignette depicts the extensive thinking-through
of the places, circumstances, and people the researchers would have to learn
about in order to respond thoughtfully and sensitively to the research
questions.

Vignette 10
___

Sampling People and Behaviors

To plan for the study, the researchers identified those events, settings,
actors, and artifacts that would have the greatest potential to yield good
data on each of five cultural domains: collegiality, community, goals and
expectations, action orientation, and knowledge base for teaching. Items
within each category provided parameters to frame data collection and
represented the core data the researchers believed would be useful. See

Table 3.3   Data Collection—Sampling

	Collegiality	Community	Goals and Expectations	Action Orientation	Knowledge Base
Settings					
public places (main office, hallways)					
teachers' lounge or lunchroom	x	x			
classrooms		x	x	x	x
meeting rooms	x		x	x	x
private offices					
counselor's		x	x		
disciplinarian's		x	x		
vice principal for scheduling's			x		
coaches'		x	x		
principal's			x		
department office or workroom	x		x	x	x
gymnasium or locker room		x	x		
auditorium		x			
Events					
events during which professionals interact					
faculty/department meetings	x		x		x
lunch/coffee break/recess	x	x			x
in-service sessions	x				x
after school (the local pub?)	x	x			
events during which professionals and students interact					
teaching acts		x	x	x	x
extracurricular activities		x	x	x	
suspensions and expulsions		x	x	x	
roster changes		x	x	x	
crisis counseling		x	x	x	
assemblies and pep rallies		x	x	x	

(continued)

Table 3.3 for the framework in which the potential usefulness of each item for the five domains was assessed.

The researchers started with *settings* because these were the most concrete—a synonym for settings is *places*. During the first few weeks in the field, they planned to collect data in the public places (main office, hallways, parking lot); the teachers' lounge or lunchroom; classrooms;

Table 3.3   Continued

	1	2	3	4	5
Actors					
administrators					
principal			x	x	x
vice principal for discipline		x	x		
vice principal for curriculum	x		x	x	x
vice principal for schedule/roster		x	x		
vice principal for activities					
counselors		x	x		
coaches		x	x		
teachers					
department heads	x	x	x	x	x
different tenure in building	x	x	x	x	x
different departments	x	x	x	x	x
students					
different ability levels		x	x		
different visibility		x	x		
Artifacts					
documents					
newspapers		x	x		x
policy statements			x	x	x
attendance records		x	x		
disciplinary records		x	x		
achievement test scores			x		
objects					
logos	x	x			
mascots	x	x			
trophies			x		
decorations		x			
art work		x			
physical arrangements	x	x			

SOURCE: Rossman, Corbett, and Firestone (1984, p. 54). Reprinted by permission.

meeting rooms; in private offices; department offices or workrooms; the gymnasium or locker room; and the auditorium.

In each of these settings, certain *events* of interest would likely occur. For example, in the disciplinarian's office there would be the handling of routine infractions, suspensions, or expulsions; in the counselor's office there might be crisis interventions. Both types of events would reveal beliefs about collegiality, community, and goals and expectations. In general, the researchers expected that the events of importance would include events during which professionals interacted: formal routines like faculty/department meetings, evaluations, and union meetings; informal routines such as lunch or coffee breaks, preparation periods, recess, morning arrivals; and events during which professionals interacted with students, including teaching acts, extracurricular activities, suspensions and expulsions, roster changes, crisis counseling, postsecondary counseling, and assemblies and pep rallies.

The first category—events during which professionals interact—would provide major data on collegiality, goals and expectations, and the knowledge base for teaching. Faculty/department meetings would be crucial as teachers discussed the curriculum, testing, new state requirements, and homework policies, as well as the more mundane aspects of high school life (announcements of schedule changes, field trips, general announcements). In these meetings, norms governing the local definition of teaching and norms regarding how teachers should relate to one another in a meeting setting would be evident. Morning routines and other informal encounters would also reveal these norms, but in less structured settings. The brief encounters might contain requests for help, plans for meetings, supportive gestures, queries about how a particular concept or skill is best taught—any of these events would reflect notions of collegiality and definitions of teaching.

The second category—events during which professionals and students interact—would provide data about community, goals and expectations, and action orientation. Both in the classroom and outside, when teachers and students interacted they would reveal whether or not there was a sense of community, what their expectations were for one another regarding behavior and achievement, and whether teachers felt it was important to translate ideas and concepts into actions—lesson and courses.

As data collection progressed, the researchers wanted to be sure that they sampled the perceptions of the following *actors:* administrators including the principal and the vice principals for discipline, instruction, and scheduling; counselors; coaches; teachers; department heads; students of different ability levels and different visibility within the school; and external actors including superintendents, curriculum coordinators, board members, community members, and state education agency staff.

Finally, the researchers planned to collect or be able to describe certain artifacts that would provide data for each of the five domains. Included would be documents, school newspapers, policy statements, attendance records, disciplinary records, achievement test scores, objects, logos, mascots, trophies, decorations, and the physical arrangements of each school.

In the above plan, the emphasis was on observation because many of the domains the researchers were trying to understand were implicit. Thus they inferred norms and values from behavior patterns and from naturally occurring conversations. Interviews helped them understand the settings and reconstruct the history of change in the high schools.

The sampling plan shown in Vignette 10 tried to assure that each site's events, rituals, resources, and interactions would be observed. Although such plans are often subject to change, given the realities of field research, at the proposal stage they demonstrate that the researcher has thought through some of the complexities of the setting and has made some initial judgments about how to deploy her time. Such plans also indicate that the researcher has considered both the informational adequacy and efficiency of these methods. Related to these considerations, however, are the ethical issues of the researcher's role with participants. These issues are considered next.

The Researcher's Role: Issues of Entry, Reciprocity, Personal Biography, and Ethics

In qualitative studies, the researcher is the "instrument": Her presence in the lives of the participants invited to be part of the study is fundamental to the paradigm. Whether that presence is sustained and intensive, as in long-term ethnographies, or whether relatively brief but personal, as in in-depth interview studies, the researcher enters into the lives of the participants. This brings a range of strategic, ethical, and personal issues that do not attend quantitative approaches (Locke, Spirduso, & Silverman, 1993). The issues can be sorted into *technical* ones that address entry and efficiency in terms of role, and *interpersonal* ones that capture the ethical

and personal dilemmas that arise (always!) during the conduct of a study
(Rossman, 1984). Clearly, the considerations overlap and have reciprocal
implications; for clarity, however, each set of issues is addressed in turn.

Technical Considerations

At the proposal stage, the technical considerations addressed include
decisions about the deployment of the researcher's time and other resources, and negotiating access.

Deploying the Self. Patton (1990) develops a series of continua for thinking
about one's role in planning the conduct of qualitative research. This
section relies on that work considerably. First, the researcher may plan a
role that entails varying degrees of "participantness"—that is, the degree
of actual participation in daily life. At one extreme is the full participant,
who goes about ordinary life in a role or set of roles constructed in the
setting. At the other is the complete observer, who engages not at all in
social interaction and may even shun involvement in the world being
studied. And, of course, all possible complementary mixes along the continuum are available to the researcher.

It is our experience that some sort of participation usually becomes
necessary as the researcher helps out with small chores (or large ones),
wants to learn more about a particular activity, or feels compelled to
participate to meet the demands of reciprocity. Such interaction is usually
highly informative while remaining informal.

Next, the researcher's role may vary as to its "revealedness" or the extent
to which the fact that there is a study going on is known to the participants.
Full disclosure lies at one end of this continuum; complete secrecy lies at
the other. There is a raft of ethical issues surrounding covert research (see
Taylor & Bogdan, 1984, chap. 3, for a provocative discussion) that winnow
down to one fundamental question: Is the potential advancement of knowledge worth the deceit? Many researchers follow Taylor and Bogdan's (1984,
p. 25) advice to be "truthful but vague" in the portrayal of the research
purpose to participants. The researcher should discuss the issues around
revealing or concealing the purpose of the study.

Third, the researcher's role may vary in intensiveness and extensiveness,
that is, the amount of time spent in the setting on a daily basis and the
duration of the study over time. Various positions on both dimensions

demand certain role considerations on the part of the researcher. For example, an intensive and extensive study requires the researcher to devote considerable time early on to developing trusting relations with the participants. Gathering pertinent data is secondary at that point. On the other hand, when the researcher will be minimally intrusive and present for a short period of time, building trusting relations must proceed in conjunction with gathering good data. In our view, this is difficult for novice researchers to accomplish.

Finally, the researcher's role may vary depending on the focus of the study: specific or diffuse. When the research questions are well developed beforehand and the data appropriate to address those questions have been identified, the researcher's role will be managed efficiently and carefully to ensure good use of the available time (both the researcher's and the setting participants'). Even when well specified, however, sound qualitative design protects the researcher's right to follow the compelling question, the nagging puzzle that presents itself once in the setting. When the research questions are more diffuse and exploratory, the plan for deploying the self should ensure access to a number of events, people, and perspectives on the social phenomenon chosen for study.

Fortunately, some researchers who have used participant observation have provided extensive descriptions of their plans, rationales, and actual experiences. Notable among these are researchers who have engaged in significant reflection on the research endeavor and their lives as researchers. These include, for example, Eisner's *The Enlightened Eye* (1991); Geertz's *Works and Lives: The Anthropologist as Author* (1988); Piotrkowski's *Work and the Family System: A Naturalistic Study of Working-Class and Lower-Middle-Class Families* (1979); Van Maanen, *Tales of the Field: On Writing Ethnography* (1988); and W. F. Whyte, *Learning From the Field: A Guide From Experience* (1984). Also recommended for further reading on this subject are Glesne and Peshkin (1992), Jorgensen (1989), and Patton (1990), among others.

Negotiating Entry. The research design section of a proposal should contain plans for negotiating access to the site and/or participants through formal and informal gatekeepers in an organization, whether the organization is an urban gang or an Ivy League university. Instead of controlling and sanitizing their presence, qualitative researchers identify and present aspects of themselves that will be useful. The energy that comes from high personal interest (called *bias* in traditional research) is useful for gaining access. Access may be a continuous issue when the researcher moves around in various settings within an organization. The researcher should reveal a sensitivity for participants' testing and reluctance to participate, and should unquestionably respect their right not to participate in a study. Excellent discussions of issues of access can be found in general texts about qualitative research such as Bogdan and Biklen (1992); Eisner (1991); Patton (1990); Schwartz and Jacobs (1979); and Taylor and Bogdan (1984). Of particular interest is Anderson's (1976) experience in becoming accepted for an ethnographic study of an urban cultural group, detailed in Vignette 11.

Vignette 11

Negotiating Entry

A bleak corner of urban life. A bar and liquor store named Jelly's that also serves as a hangout for African-American men in south Chicago. In such a place an angry man pulls a knife on another, a wino sleeps off his last bottle, police cars cruise without stopping, all taking place within the sight of children at play. Jelly's and its countless urban counterparts "provide settings for sociability and places where neighborhood residents can gain a sense of self worth" (Anderson, 1976, p. 1).

Anderson determined that he was going to study this particular setting, but how was he to gain entry? His first observations indicated that "visitors" received special treatment, because the next person might prove to be "the police," "the baddest cat in Chicago," or someone waiting to follow another home and rip him off. In the words of the regular clientele at Jelly's, "unknown people bear watching" (Anderson, 1976, p. 5).

Anderson accepted visitor treatment for several weeks, being unobtrusive yet sociable, acquainting himself with the unwritten social rules. Being African American was insufficient justification for immediate acceptance by the "regulars." Enter Herman. Anderson cultivated a relationship with Herman that became a means for mutual protection of each other's "rep and rank" in the social status system at Jelly's. Anderson responded openly to Herman's persistent questioning, and several days later, Herman reciprocated by introducing Anderson to Sleepy, T J, and Jake. "He all right. Hey this is the study I been tellin' you about. This cat getting his doctor's degree." With this introduction to the regulars, Anderson's place in the social system had been defined. In short, it provided Anderson with a license to be around. Herman used Anderson to gain credibility at his on-the-job Christmas party, introducing Anderson as "cousin" and getting him to tell the regulars at Jelly's how well Herman got along with "decent folks and intelligent folks" (p. 20).

Anderson's role evolved naturally from the low-key, nonassertive role he initially assumed to prevent unwieldy challenges from those who might have felt threatened by a more aggressive demeanor, especially from a stranger. It is the kind of role any outsider must play—is forced into—if he is not to disrupt "the consensual definition of social order in this type of setting" (pp. 22-23).

Anderson's experience is typical of those proposing long-term ethnographic studies of particular groups. At times the best entry is one, like this one, where there is an insider who provides sponsorship and helps the researcher seem nonthreatening. There are circumstances, however, when sponsorship can backfire, setting the researcher up for difficulties in accessing other groups within the organization. For those conducting studies of organizations, negotiating access may require perseverance and persistence with formal leaders within the organization, as Vignette 12 depicts.

Vignette 12

Persistence

Negotiating access for the conduct of the long-term study of culture and change in three American high schools (Rossman et al., 1988) proved challenging in one instance, taking more than 3 months for formal approval of the study. Events unfolded as follows. First, a letter was sent to the principal, briefly describing the study. During a follow-up telephone conversation, a meeting was scheduled at which the principal was to meet with two researchers. This meeting was difficult because the principal challenged the notion of "culture" as being meaningful for schools. The researchers felt defensive. One of the researchers, moreover, had no professional experience in schools and felt vulnerable on that count.

A second meeting and then a third were scheduled. The second was with members of the teachers' union; the third was with the entire faculty. At both meetings, the researchers were asked questions about their intentions, their credibility, their presentability, and their knowledge of schools and schooling. Finally, after the third meeting, the faculty voted to participate in the study. This was the climate that had been established before Rossman began data collection. A somewhat suspicious faculty had agreed to do the study. Establishing credibility and winning over the power structure in the school were the first research tasks.

Gaining access to sites—receiving formal approval—requires time, patience, and sensitivity to the rhythms and norms of a group. At the proposal stage, the researcher should indicate that negotiations have begun and formal approval is likely or that she has knowledge about the nuances of entry and a healthy respect for participants' concerns.

Efficiency. In qualitative studies the researcher should think through how he will deploy the resources available for the study to ensure full responses to the research questions. Although this consideration overlaps directly with decisions about data gathering, issues of role also arise here. The researcher should think through carefully how he can deploy the self, as it were, to maximize the opportunities for gathering data. This consideration should be balanced against the resources available for the study, however, most notably time and energy. We would caution the novice, moreover, that once a study is begun the tantalizing puzzles and intriguing questions mushroom. Even though the researcher reserves the right to pursue those, he should remain mindful of the goal of the project. Doctoral students often need to be gently prodded back into a structure for the completion of the work. Also, a priori but tentative statements about delimitations will help: A discussion of goals and limitations (e.g., five life histories; observations in one school for one year) and reminders of practical considerations (e.g., dwindling funds) serve as reminders that the research must be finite.

Interpersonal Considerations

One could argue that successful qualitative studies depend primarily on the interpersonal skills of the researcher. In general texts this is often couched as *building trust, maintaining good relations,* respecting *norms of reciprocity,* and sensitively considering *ethical issues.* These entail an awareness of the politics of organizations, as well as a sensitivity to human interaction. Because the conduct of the study often depends exclusively on the relationships the researcher builds with participants, interpersonal skills are paramount. We would go so far as to dissuade a would-be qualitative researcher from this approach if she did not possess the skills of easily conversing with others, being an active and thoughtful listener, and having empathetic understanding of and a profound respect for the perspectives of others. It is important to acknowledge that some people just cannot be good qualitative researchers.

Discussions of one's role in the setting and consideration of how this may affect participants' willingness to engage in thoughtful reflection help provide evidence that the researcher knows enough about the setting and the people, their routines, and their environments to anticipate how she will fit in. Researchers benefit from carefully thinking through their roles, because most participants detect and reject insincere, unauthentic people.

In addition, researchers may have to *teach* the participants what the researcher's role is. They should describe their likely activities while in the setting, what they are interested in learning about, the possible uses of the information, and how the participants can engage in the research. Norms of reciprocity suggest that the researcher cannot be simply a spongelike observer, as Thorne (1983) describes in compelling detail in her reflections on studying war resistance in the 1960s, because many people will not respond to or trust someone who will not take a stand. Two vignettes provide further illustration of these ideas. Vignette 13 describes how Rosalie Wax (1971) went about the complex task of building trust in her study of Native Americans; Vignette 14 provides an example of planning to manage the political issues on a site.

Vignette 13
___

Building Trust

The extensive writing of anthropologist Rosalie Wax (1971) has emphasized the importance of the researcher's initial contacts with the members of the society or group chosen for study. The reciprocal relationship between host and field-worker enables the latter to avoid foolish, insulting, and potentially dangerous behavior; to make valuable contacts; and to understand the acceptance and repayment of obligations. "The most egregious error that a fieldworker can commit," according to Wax (1971, p. 47), is assuming that tolerance by hosts also implies their high regard and inclusion.

In her ethnographic community study of Native American reservation society, Wax found the women embarrassed and hesitant to open their poor, bare homes to the scrutiny of a researcher. Their trust and cooperation were essential to her study because Wax sought to understand the relationship between cultural patterns expressed in the home and poor school adjustment and underachievement of the children. In her account of the slow uncovering of answers, Wax reveals her method of making others comfortable with her presence. She permitted children to play with her typewriter. She employed some of the women as interviewers. Avoiding the social worker or Bureau of Indian Affairs do-gooder image, Wax interacted as woman to woman, always exploring but doing so with an interest in the welfare of the women's children.

Vignette 13 demonstrates that researchers should be sensitive to the need for time to pass, flexibility in their roles, and patience, because confidence and trust emerge over time through complex interactions. Roles and relationships *do* emerge in the field. At the proposal stage, however, the researcher should demonstrate a logical plan that respects the need for time to build relationships. It is not enough to state that trust and relationships are important. The researcher should also display the skills and sensitivities to deal with complexities in relationships that inevitably emerge during fieldwork. Vignette 14 illustrates how role maintenance and management were crucial during the conduct of the high school cultures study and illustrates the potential difficulties of sponsorship through the existing power structures (discussed above).

Vignette 14

Managing the Political

During the conduct of a long-term study of culture and change in three American high schools (Rossman et al., 1988), one of the

researchers encountered role management dilemmas that threatened her
continued access to members of the high school community. As
described above (see Vignette 12), negotiating access had been a long,
drawn-out process as participants quite legitimately questioned what
was in it for them, the researcher's credibility, and discussed the
intrusion into their lives.

Given the challenges to her presence in the school, Rossman spent
considerable time early on with the principal and his close associates,
learning about their values and beliefs about the school and the children,
building trust, and observing how power and influence were expressed
through that small group of people. Six weeks into the study, Rossman
decided to gather data systematically from each department in the
school. This would necessitate distancing herself from the principal and
his close associates, although she felt it would be wise to continue to
"check in" with them on a regular basis. Through contact with each
department head, Rossman scheduled interviews and observations with
several teachers representing the various subject matter specializations.
As data gathering sped up, Rossman felt she could spend less and less
time with the administrators and their associates. As she distanced
herself from them and spent more time with teachers in the lunchroom,
in their classrooms, in the hallways, and after school, however, she found
that the principal and his associates increasingly questioned her as to her
whereabouts and what she was learning from the teachers.

The school had been through a series of traumatic events 4 years prior
to the study and, some believed, was still reeling. During that time,
teachers and administrators formed two camps, each claiming that its
views were true and proper. Rossman surmised that the principal was
still concerned over those historic events and wanted to keep her from
learning about those times or, barring that, at least to ensure that she
heard a balanced presentation.

Rossman's dilemma was this: She could cater to the principal and his
associates, being sure that they knew her activities each day and could
keep track of her comings and goings. This continued close association
with the power structure, however, might work against building trust
with teachers, especially those who might have been involved in the
earlier traumatic times. Would those teachers trust her after seeing her
so closely associated with the principal? On the other hand, the principal
controlled access to the high school: Without his permission, the study

could end. Without his support and confidence in the researcher, the climate in which the study proceeded could become strained, at best.

Recognizing the dilemma, Rossman tried to balance the competing concerns. She made a point of checking into the main office each day. There she would tell the head secretary, one of the assistant principals, or another of the principal's close associates her general "itinerary" for the day. Having done that (in cheerful tones and with expressions such as, "if anyone needs to reach me, I'll be with the English department today"), she felt comfortable moving out into the school to uncover teachers' perspectives on the nature of the work and the social relations there. Although relations were never quite as smooth with the principal, this strategy helped protect the study from excessive scrutiny and ensured continued access to the remainder of the teachers.

Tensions do arise when researchers are involved over the long term, and researchers must plan strategies for easing those tensions. Researchers may also need to think about strategies to maintain the research instrument, that is, the self. Research designs should include strategies to protect the physical and emotional health and safety of the researcher by providing plans for quiet places in which he can write notes, reassess roles, retreat from the setting, or question the directions of the research. In doing so, proposals should cite the experiences of previous researchers and apply them to the current research to think through role strategies. Everhart (1977), Glesne (1989), Krieger (1985), Peshkin (1988), and Thorne (1983) provide thought-provoking discussions; more classical works are those of Bowen (1964) and Olesen and Whittaker (1967a), among others. Moving on to another site is another way to manage—politically and ethically—a difficult situation: There are times when, even with the best planning, the researcher cannot gain entry to a site, as Vignette 15 shows.

Vignette 15
_____

Moving On

Wanting to explore the interaction between community political demands and women and people of color's access to school district leadership, Marshall (1992) designed comparative case studies and identified two sites—two cities in the same region of the country with similar political cultures, demographic composition, and comparatively large numbers of women and people of color in leadership positions. The sites were chosen for comparability along those dimensions but with one significant difference: "Change City" showed evidence of a political structure undergoing substantial change, whereas "Avondale" represented a more placid political climate. She crafted the following letter as a way of introducing herself and the study to important gatekeepers in the districts:

Dear _____,

The purpose of this letter is to introduce myself and to ask you to please consider the possibility of allowing me to collect research data within your school system. I am enclosing my résumé. I am presently an Associate Professor within the Department of Educational Leadership at Vanderbilt University. I have done extensive research on women and minorities within the field of educational administration.

This is a field research project in which I and two other researchers will visit administrators on-site to observe the activities of women or minority principals. All individuals and sites involved in this study will remain anonymous. I assure you that I will respect your need as superintendent to minimize politically sensitive issues. Consequently, the complete research will be published only in a professional journal.

I am conducting a long-term research project on school districts with large numbers of women and minority administrators. With your permission, I would like to conduct this research in [____]. Enclosed you will find a copy of the entire research proposal that I think you will find quite interesting.

Briefly, the focus of the study is the interaction of school district policy and successful incorporation of women and minorities within the administrative ranks, particularly within the principalship. [____] was chosen because of the changes you are implementing at the administrative level. You stand out for taking strong action to rethink the principalship.

I would enjoy discussing this project with you on the telephone. I will contact your secretary during the week of April 23, 1990, to arrange a phone conversation with you at your convenience. Thank you for your time and consideration in this matter.

Sincerely,

At Avondale, Marshall encountered no more than the typical bureaucratic barriers to gaining access: letters to gatekeepers, meetings with district research directors, assurances of compliance with district monitoring of the research. Pleased with this response, she began the access process in Change City by subscribing to the local newspaper to learn about local politics and by placing phone calls to the superintendent, a newly hired African-American man from another state. Weeks passed. Months passed. Her politely persistent calls resulted in a telephone relationship with the secretary! She devised other strategies: letters flattering to the superintendent, reassurances of the value of the research for the district, name-dropping, emphasizing the university letterhead and the study's connection to a national center on school leadership. Still no response.

Marshall found this puzzling, because superintendents are known to try to maintain at least diplomatic relationships with university faculty. It was also humiliating, because Marshall saw herself as somewhat expert at gaining access to policy settings, encouraging state officials to tell her insider stories, and getting past bureaucratic barriers (Marshall, 1984).

In conversations with a doctoral student with some connections to the new superintendent of Change City, Marshall searched for insights only to learn that this new superintendent was judicious with his time and extremely careful about controlling information as he dealt with an explosive dispute about resources, people of color in administrative positions, and political maneuvers to support incumbent white administrators. No wonder he was wary!

Intrigued with this turmoil and hungry to know more because it spoke so directly to the research topic, Marshall tried one last tactic: the "chance" meeting. With a little help from the superintendent's secretary, she learned of a small conference that the superintendent planned to attend, got herself invited, and was able to engage him in conversation during a coffee break. In the context of conference-related talk, she mentioned casually that she hoped to talk with him about doing research in the district. Gracious, interested, and promising to talk at length at the next break, the superintendent appeared open. One hour later, much to Marshall's chagrin, his assistant announced that the superintendent had been called back to the office to manage some emergency. Foiled again!

Marshall resumed the phone calls and letters with the added hint that the superintendent had promised a longer conversation. The silence from his office was deafening. It was time to let go of her pride and face facts. The political controversies about people of color in leadership positions—the very question that she wanted to study—was the tense and difficult issue that had this superintendent embroiled. It was clear that he was not about to risk the exposure of this political maelstrom through qualitative research. Marshall went back to the library to find another "Change City."

It is hard to admit that the original plan will not work. Sometimes, because the politics in a setting are so explosive, researchers must simply move on. At some point they decide that the efforts to get around the barriers to entry are excessive, and they must respect the needs of key actors in the setting. With topics that are politicized and sensitive, the researcher can identify several potential sites so she can move to another site easily if one will not work. When one site will not work, the researcher can then move to an alternative with little delay.

Reciprocity and Ethics. A thorough research proposal also demonstrates the researcher's awareness of reciprocity issues. Qualitative studies intrude into settings as people adjust to the researcher's presence. People may be giving their time to be interviewed or to help the researcher understand group norms; the researcher should plan to reciprocate. Where people adjust their priorities and routines to help the researcher, or even just tolerate the researcher's presence, they are giving of themselves. The researcher is indebted and should be sensitive to this. Reciprocity may entail giving time to help out, providing informal feedback, making coffee, being a good listener, or tutoring. Of course, reciprocity should fit within the constraints of research and personal ethics, and within the constraints of maintaining one's role as a researcher role.

Ethics. The qualities that make a successful qualitative researcher should be revealed through an exquisite sensitivity to the ethical issues that are present when we engage in any moral act. Ethical considerations are generic—such as informed consent and protecting participants' anonymity—as well as situation-specific. Several authors discuss ethical considerations in the conduct of qualitative research, describing the dilemmas they have encountered. Particularly noteworthy are the works of Emerson (1983), Galliher (1983), Punch (1986), Van Maanen (1983), and Wax (1983). Role, reciprocity, and ethics issues must be thought through carefully in all settings but most particularly in sensitive and taboo areas, as detailed in Vignette 16.

Vignette 16

Role and Reciprocity

How do researchers go about gaining the confidence of persons involved in illegal activities in order to make data collection about such activities possible? True and True (1977) detailed the system of reciprocity that made possible their study of drug use in San Jose, Costa Rica. Operating out of the established premise that the forms and meanings of drug use emerge from the sociocultural context, the research examined the use of marijuana among working-class men by doing extensive sociocultural and biomedical studies of a matched sample of 41 users and 41 nonusers.

For 14 months, a networking approach was employed in the recruitment of a base sample of 240 subjects and the selection of the final matched sample. Recruitment proved difficult because of the severe penalties for marijuana use or suspected sale, the conspicuousness of a large police force devoted to the control of narcotics trafficking, and the highly refined evasive skills of users who suspected that a stranger might have connections with the police. Initial attempts to identify productive locations for recruitment proved unfruitful. With persistence, however, some locations were discovered: a park corner, a bar, a particular street corner, a shoe shop, and an athletic field. The researchers frequented these sites for a few months, working to establish a core of contacts who, noting that no police harassment followed them, would vouch for the fact that the researchers were no INTERPOL officers.

Confidentiality was only one of the factors figuring into the reciprocal relationships that enabled data collection. The researchers also gave of their time. They became full participants in the social life of their contacts. They visited in homes and became involved in family activities. They spent time in conversations on the street corner, in bars and cafes, and in workplaces. They participated in recreational outings, community activities, and soccer games, often being the ones responsible for providing transportation.

The researchers served as intermediaries between the men and such institutions as the Ministry of Security. When feasible, the researchers made personal loans, purchased food, and paid overdue rent. When the medical screening of the base sample of 240 was completed, the researchers used their official status with the Ministry of Health to arrange for medical services. In return, the men granted informed consent to participate in extensive medical, neuropsychological, and sociocultural studies. As a result of the rapport that was established, the researchers were the recipients of candid life narratives that thoroughly detailed the drug histories of their interviewees. The participants also reciprocated through their acceptance of the delicate balance between participants and formal institutions that had to be maintained by the researchers. Although abuse during police interrogations was alleged by participants, they did not expect the researchers to take on the Ministry of Security and thus risk the future of the project.

The careful attention that was given to reciprocity in the researchers' relationships with participants contributed significantly to the success of this particular study.

The vignettes have shown the importance of planning and drawing on the experience of previous researchers. The competent research proposal, then, anticipates issues of negotiating entry, reciprocity, role maintenance, and receptivity, but, at the same time, it must adhere to ethical principles. The researcher must demonstrate awareness of the complex ethical issues in qualitative research and show that the research is both feasible and ethical. If the researcher will be playing a deceptive role, she should demonstrate that this will not be harmful to the participants in the research. If the researcher will require people to change their routines or donate their time, it must be voluntary. What is routine and acceptable in one setting may be harmful in another; what is volunteered in one may be forced in another. The researcher cannot anticipate everything, but she must reveal an awareness and appreciation of and commitment to ethical principles for research. Several authors have explored these issues in both general texts and articles. We recommend Emerson (1983), Rist (1981), and Spradley (1979), as well as the following vignettes.

Vignette 17

Ethics and Ethnographic Fieldwork

Ethnographic research has traditionally been undertaken in fields that, by virtue of the contrast between them and the researcher's own culture, could be described as "exotic." The researcher's goal is to describe the symbols and values of such a culture without passing judgment based upon his personal cultural context. Soloway and Walters (1977), however, point out that when a researcher studies those whose acts are considered criminal, profound ethical dilemmas arise: "When one decides to attempt to enter their world and to study it, the fieldworker arrives at a true moral, ethical, and legal existential crisis" (p. 161).

Though researchers are expected to suspend judgment even when investigating one of the dark fissures of their own culture, it is often very difficult to do so. Soloway and Walters (1977) assert that: "The failure of urban anthropological studies of modern American culture is that this critical phenomenological judgment has not been substantially dealt with by urban anthropologists in any meaningful way" (p. 161).

One option is to carry out studies of criminal subcultures from within institutions, such as prisons or treatment centers. Critical of such a procedure, Soloway and Walters note that, "if addicts are studied at Lexington [federal hospital], then the result is a study of patients. If addicts are studied in jail, the result is a study of prisoners" (p. 163).

In order to understand addiction, Soloway chose to enter the addicts' natural habitat. Entry was aided by his affiliation with a methadone treatment program and the fact that he was doing his research within the neighborhood where he had spent his childhood. One of his contacts during observation of the weekly distribution of methadone was Mario, an old neighborhood friend and a patient at the treatment center.

Mario saw this relationship as a source of status both within the program and on the street. He chose to test this relationship at one point, coming in high for his weekly dose. When he was refused the methadone because of his condition, he sought out his friend the ethnographer to intercede with the nurses. Not only did the researcher refuse to intercede, he rebuked Mario, saying, "I'm no lame social worker from the suburbs; you're high and everybody knows it. Now stop being such a c—-!" (Soloway & Walters, 1977, p. 165). Even though he risked jeopardizing the researcher-informant relationship, the risk paid off. Mario eventually introduced Soloway to other addicts; this involvement with urban heroin addicts enabled him to observe them in the context of their total social milieu, where "junkie" was only part of their identity.

Was Soloway taking advantage of his friendship with Mario? Is the participant observer a friend to his subjects? Can the researcher be both observer and friend? How does one juggle the objectivity of the stranger and the friend's desires for the well-being of a friend? "The bind on the ethnographer's personal ethic is," according to Soloway and Walters, "that his total integrity cannot be maintained in either role" (p. 166). What represents a researcher's ethical response when observing or possibly becoming involved in criminal activity? Polsky (1969) insists that in order to study adult criminals in their natural settings, one must "make the moral decision that in some ways he will break the law himself" (pp. 133-134). On the other hand, Yablonsky (1965) asserts that participant observation among the criminally deviant merely serves, by way of the researcher's interest in the subject, to reinforce the criminal behavior.

In the exchange with Mario, the researcher attempted to strike a balance by employing the principle of relativism. According to this principle, ethnographers are not expected to renounce their own culturally formed consciences, nor are they to project those values on their subjects. "Relativism operationally guards against two dangers, the ethnographer's own ethnocentrism and an equally dangerous inverted ethnocentrism—i.e., going native and personally identifying with the studied value system" (Soloway & Walters, 1977, p. 168). Not all qualitative studies present such extreme ethical dilemmas. It is, however, quite difficult to maintain the role of researcher when caught in the middle of events that seem to call for action, as the next vignette shows.

Vignette 18

Ensuring Ethical Behavior

Persons engaged in criminal acts are not likely to be open to completing a questionnaire about those activities. Because of this, qualitative approaches to research are often found in areas that extend beyond the parameters of either legality or morality. Doing observation and interviewing in such settings has presented and will continue to present field-workers with ethical dilemmas. What does the researcher do in the presence of illegal activities? Is the researcher's primary responsibility to the research task, to those being observed, to those assisting with the observation, or to society as a whole? When initiating entry into a field of research, can the researcher offer guarantees that her behavior will conform to specific ethical standards?

Manning's (1972) research into police work—primarily that of narcotics officers—demonstrates the ethical dilemmas faced by some field-workers. The researcher's role is limited—he may walk the beat with the police officer, ride in the patrol car with the police officer, even tag along when an arrest is about to be made. Yet the researcher cannot be a police officer, cannot wear the uniform, cannot take the risks, cannot make the arrests, cannot adopt the police officer's perspective. He also cannot be a criminal. What then?

Manning points out the contrast between the police officer and the researcher. The role of the former "seems to attract men who are apparently deeply ambivalent about the law, politically conservative, perhaps reactionary, and persons of lower- or lower-middle-class origins with a high school or less education" (p. 244). The social scientist, on the other hand, "tends to be politically liberal, of middle-class origins, highly educated, and intellectual" (p. 244). How do researchers go about courting the cooperation of individuals whose social ecology is so very different from their own? Must researchers assume identities other than their own? According to Westley (1967), a critical "norm" among law enforcement personnel is the maintenance of secrecy:

> It is carefully taught to every rookie policeman; it is observed by all the men, and there are powerful sanctions against its violation. . . . The violator is cut off from vital sources of information and the protection of his colleagues in times of emergency. . . . Secrecy means that policemen must not talk about police work to those outside the department. (p. 774)

Strike two. The researcher not only differs from the police officer in terms of social milieu, but, along with anyone else asking lots of questions or appearing too curious, is simply not wanted.

The seemingly innocent act of encouraging police officers to talk about their work may jeopardize their professional relationships as well as their safety. How ethical are such actions? What of the issue of the "watched cop" raised by Manning? Is it possible for police officers to be effective when they are aware of the fact that observation is taking place or when constrained by the need to keep in mind the safety of the researcher?

Manning extends the dilemma by referring to a researcher who observed a clear incidence of police brutality and who knew that the officer involved was aware of his observations. The researcher debated the pros and cons of complying with the law and turning the officer in, risking the destruction of the study, and remaining silent in order to gain the trust of those he was observing along with some leverage for later on. Manning contrasts this student—who opted for the benefits of silence—with another from the same project who, having observed a case of a police officer harassing blacks in an inner-city area, "indignantly reported the event [and] was banned from further observation" (pp. 251-252).

Although Vignette 18 describes quite dramatic dilemmas, researchers must anticipate more routine ethical issues and be prepared to make on-the-spot decisions that (hopefully) follow general ethical principles (see Spradley, 1980). Reading other researchers' discussions of ethical problems and dealing with hypothetical situations through case material can illuminate more "standard" ethical considerations (although no ethical problem is truly unique), and refine the researcher's abilities to reason through moral argumentation.

The above discussions have taken the reader through the messy process of deciding on an overall approach to the study, building a rationale around it, discussing the site or participants, and thinking about their role and ethics in the conduct of the study. The next chapter describes an array of primary and supplementary data collection methods—the concrete answers to the "how will I do this study" question.

4 Data Collection Methods

The fundamental methods relied on by qualitative researchers for gathering information are (1) participation in the setting, (2) direct observation, (3) in-depth interviewing, and (4) document review. These methods form the core, the staples of the diet. Supplementing these are several specialized methods. This chapter provides a discussion of both the primary and secondary methods for consideration in designing a qualitative study.

Primary Methods

Participation

Developed mainly through the disciplines of cultural anthropology and qualitative sociology, participant observation (as this method is typically called) is both an overall approach to inquiry and a data gathering method. Participant observation is to some degree an essential element of all qualitative studies. As its name reveals, participant observation demands firsthand involvement in the social world chosen for study. Immersion in the setting allows the researcher to hear, see, and begin to experience reality as the participants do. Ideally, the researcher spends a considerable amount of time in the setting, learning about daily life.

This method for gathering data is basic to all qualitative studies and forces a discussion of the role or stance of the researcher as a participant observer. Issues of role have been explored more fully in a previous section; we reiterate here that, at the proposal stage, it is helpful to elaborate the planned extent of participation, what the nature of that participation is likely to be, how much will be revealed about the study's purpose to the people in the setting, how intensive the participation will be, and how focused the participation will be. Full discussions of participant observation are found in the classical work of Pelto and Pelto (1978) and Spradley (1980), as well as the more current work of Jorgensen (1989) and Van Manen (1990). All general texts, moreover, discuss participant observation.

Observation

Observation entails the systematic noting and recording of events, behaviors, and artifacts (objects) in the social setting chosen for study. For studies relying exclusively on observation, the researcher makes no special effort to have a particular role; to be tolerated as an unobtrusive observer is often enough. Classroom observational studies are one example often found in education. Through observation, the researcher learns about behaviors and the meanings attached to those behaviors. This method assumes that behavior is purposive and expressive of deeper values and beliefs. Observation can range from highly structured, detailed notation of behavior guided by checklists to more holistic description of events and behavior.

In the early stages of qualitative inquiry, the researcher typically enters the setting with broad areas of interest but without predetermined categories or strict observational checklists. The value here is that the researcher is able to discover the recurring patterns of behavior and relationships. After such patterns are identified and described through early analysis of field notes, checklists become more appropriate and context-sensitive. Focused observation then is used at later stages of the study, usually to check analytic themes to see, for example, if they explain behavior and relationships over a long time or in a variety of settings.

Observation is a fundamental and critical method in all qualitative inquiry: It is used to discover complex interactions in natural social settings. Even in in-depth interview studies, observation plays an important role as the researcher notes body language and affect in addition to the person's words. It is, however, a method that requires a great deal of the researcher. Discomfort, uncomfortable ethical dilemmas and even danger, the difficulty of managing a relatively unobtrusive role, and the challenge to identify the "big picture" while finely observing huge amounts of fast-moving and complex behavior are just a few of the challenges. An excellent discussion of observation as both overall approach and specific method is found in Evertson and Green (1985).

In-Depth Interviewing

In-depth interviewing is a data collection method relied on quite extensively by qualitative researchers. Described as, "a conversation with a purpose" (Kahn & Cannell, 1957, p. 149), in-depth interviewing may be the overall strategy or one of several methods employed in a study. Interviewing varies in terms of a priori structure and in the latitude the interviewee has in responding to questions. Patton (1990, pp. 280-290) categorizes interviews into three general types: the informal conversational interview, the general interview guide approach, and the standardized open-ended interview.

Typically, qualitative in-depth interviews are much more like conversations than formal events with predetermined response categories. The researcher explores a few general topics to help uncover the participant's meaning perspective, but otherwise respects how the participant frames and structures the responses. This, in fact, is an assumption fundamental to qualitative research—the participant's perspective on the phenomenon of interest should unfold as the participant views it, not as the researcher views it. A degree of systematization in questioning may be necessary in, for example, a multisite case study or when many participants are interviewed. The most important aspect of the interviewer's approach concerns conveying an attitude of acceptance—that the participant's information is valuable and useful. This may, however, evoke ethical dilemmas for the interviewer; we discuss these more fully below.

Interviews have particular strengths. An interview is a useful way to get large amounts of data quickly. When more than one person participates (e.g., focus group interviews, discussed below), the interview process gathers a wide variety of information across a larger number of subjects than if there were fewer participants—the familiar trade-off between breadth and depth. Immediate follow-up and clarification are possible. Combined with observation, interviews allow the researcher to understand the meanings people hold for their everyday activities.

Interviewing has limitations and weaknesses, however. Interviews involve personal interaction; cooperation is essential. Interviewees may be unwilling or uncomfortable sharing all that the interviewer hopes to explore, or they may be unaware of recurring patterns in their lives. The interviewer may not ask questions that evoke long narratives from participants either because of a lack of expertise or familiarity with local language or because of lack of skill. By the same token, responses to the questions or elements of the conversation may not be properly comprehended by the interviewer. And, at times, interviewees may have good reason not to be truthful (see Douglas, 1976, for a discussion).

Interviewers should have superb listening skills and be skillful at personal interaction, question framing, and gentle probing for elaboration. Volumes of data can be obtained through interviewing, but the data are time-consuming to analyze. Finally, there is the issue of the quality of the data. When interviews are used as the sole way of gathering data, the researcher should have demonstrated through the conceptual framework that the purpose of the study is to uncover and describe the participants' perspectives on events; that is, that the subjective view is what matters. Studies making more objective assumptions would triangulate interview data with data gathered through other methods.

For further reading on the subject of in-depth interviewing as a qualitative data collection method, see McCracken (1988), Patton (1990, chap. 7), and Tripp (1983), as well as the general texts. In addition to generic in-depth interviewing are several more specialized forms of interviews including ethnographic interviewing, phenomenological interviewing, elite interviewing, and focus group interviewing. Each is described briefly next.

Ethnographic Interviewing. Based on the discipline of cognitive anthropology, ethnographic interviewing elicits the cognitive structures guiding participants' worldviews. Described as "a particular kind of speech event" (Spradley, 1979, p. 18), ethnographic questions are used by the ethnographer to gather cultural data. Spradley (1979) identifies three main types of questions: descriptive, structural, and contrast. Descriptive questions allow the researcher to collect a sample of the participant's language. Structural questions discover the basic units in that cultural knowledge; and contrast questions provide the ethnographer with the meaning of various terms in the participant's language.

The value of the ethnographic interview lies in its focus on culture through the participant's perspective and through a firsthand encounter. This approach is especially useful for eliciting participant' meanings for events and behaviors, and generates a typology of cultural classification schemes. It also highlights the nuances of the culture. The method is flexible in formulating hypotheses and avoids oversimplification in description and analysis because of the rich narrative descriptions.

There are weaknesses in this method, however. Values may be imposed by the ethnographer. If the member of the cultural group chosen to participate does not represent that culture, the subsequent analysis will be impoverished. The success of this method, as in all interviewing, is highly dependent upon the skills of the researcher. In addition to Spradley's (1979) work on this topic, Filstead (1970) and Wolcott (1985) provide further information.

Phenomenological Interviewing. Phenomenological interviewing is a specific type of in-depth interviewing grounded in the theoretical tradition of phenomenology. Phenomenology is the study of experiences and the ways in which we put them together to develop a worldview. It carries an assumption that there is a "structure and essence" to shared experiences that can be determined (Patton, 1990, p. 70). This theoretical orientation has two implications, such that phenomenology can be referred to *either* as the subject matter of inquiry *or* as the methodology of the study.

Patton (1990) identifies three basic steps to phenomenological inquiry: Epoche, phenomenological reduction, and structural synthesis. *Epoche* is the period in which the researcher must examine herself in order to identify personal biases and remove all traces of personal involvement in the phenomena being studied. The purpose of this self-examination is for the researcher either to eliminate or to gain clarity from her own preconceptions, and it is part of the "ongoing analytic process rather than a single fixed event" (Patton, 1990, p. 408). *Phenomenological reduction* is the next phase, in which the researcher brackets the rest of the world and any presuppositions with which she approaches the subject of study. Its goal is to enable the researcher to identify the phenomenon in its "pure form, uncontaminated by extraneous intrusions" (Patton 1990, p. 408). The data are then clustered around invariant themes that this reduction has allowed the researcher to identify and to identify the textural portrayal of those themes. The final stage, *structural synthesis,* involves the articulation of the "bones" of the experience of the phenomenon and the description of its deep structure. In addition to Patton (1990), discussions of phenomenology can be found in Bogdan and Bicklen (1992), Bogdan and Taylor (1975), Denzin (1970, 1978) and Taylor and Bogdan (1984).

Elite Interviewing. An elite interview is a specialized case of interviewing that focuses on a particular type of interviewee. Elite individuals are considered to be the influential, the prominent, and the well-informed people in an organization or community and are selected for interviews on the basis of their expertise in areas relevant to the research.

Elite interviewing has many advantages. Valuable information can be gained from these participants because of the positions they hold in social, political, financial, or administrative realms. Elites can usually provide an overall view of an organization or its relationship to other organizations. They are more likely than other participants to be familiar with the legal and financial structures of the organization. Elites are also able to report on an organizations' policies, past histories, and future plans, from a particular perspective.

Elite interviewing also presents disadvantages. The problem of accessibility to elites is often great because they are usually busy people operating under demanding time constraints; they are also often difficult to reach. The interviewer may have to rely on sponsorship, recommendations, and introductions for assistance in making appointments with elite individuals.

Another disadvantage in interviewing elites is that the interviewer may have to adapt the planned-for structure of the interview, based on the wishes and predilections of the person interviewed. Although this is true with all in-depth interviewing, elite individuals are typically quite savvy and may resent the restrictions of narrow or ill-phrased questions. They may want an active interplay with the interviewer. Well practiced in meeting the public, an elite person may turn the interview around, thereby taking charge of it. Elites respond well to inquiries about broad areas of content and to a high proportion of intelligent, provocative, open-ended questions that allow them the freedom to use their knowledge and imagination.

In working with elites, great demands are placed on the ability of the interviewer, who must establish competence by displaying a thorough knowledge of the topic or, lacking such knowledge, by projecting an accurate conceptualization of the problem through shrewd questioning. The interviewer's hard work usually pays off, however, in the quality of information obtained. Elites often contribute insight and meaning to the interview process because they are intelligent and quick-thinking people, at home in the realm of ideas, policies, and generalizations. For more on the subject of interviewing elites, see Becker and Meyers (1974-1975), Marshall (1984), Platt (1981), and Webb and Salancik (1966).

Focus Group Interviewing. The technique of interviewing participants in focus groups comes largely from marketing research. The groups are generally composed of 7 to 10 people (although they range as small as 4 and as large as 12) who are unfamiliar to one another and have been selected because they share certain characteristics that are relevant to the question of the study. The interviewer creates a permissive environment, asking focused questions, in order to encourage discussion and the expression of differing opinions and points of view. These interviews are conducted several times with different individuals so that the researcher can identify trends in the perceptions and opinions expressed, which are revealed through careful, systematic analysis (Krueger, 1988, p. 18).

This method assumes that an individual's attitudes and beliefs do not form in a vacuum: People often need to listen to others' opinions and understandings in order to form their own. One-on-one interviews may be impoverished because the participant had not reflected on the topic and feels unprepared to respond. Often the questions in a focus group setting are deceptively simple; the trick is to promote the participants' self-disclosure through the creation of a permissive environment.

The advantages to focus group interviews are that this method is socially oriented, studying participants in a natural, real-life atmosphere (neither experimental nor the strain and artificiality of a one-on-one interview); the format allows the facilitator the flexibility to explore unanticipated issues as they arise in the discussion; the results have high face validity— because the method is readily understood, the findings appear believable; it is relatively low cost; it provides quick results; and it can increase the sample size of qualitative studies by interviewing more people at one time (Krueger, 1988, pp. 44-46).

There are, however, certain disadvantages to this method as well: The interviewer has less control over a group interview than an individual one, which can result in lost time as dead-end or irrelevant issues are discussed; the data are difficult to analyze, as context is essential to understanding the participants' comments; the method requires the use of highly trained observer-moderators; the groups can vary a great deal and can be hard to assemble; and, finally, there are logistical problems arising from the need to conduct the discussion as conducive to a conversation. For further reading on focus group interviews, see Birn, Hague, and Vangelder (1990), Krueger (1988), and Morgan (1988).

The Review of Documents

Researchers supplement participant observation, interviewing, and observation with the gathering and analyzing of documents produced in the course of everyday events. As such, the review of documents is an unobtrusive method (described below), one rich in portraying the values and beliefs of participants in the setting. Minutes of meetings, logs, announcements, formal policy statements, letters, and so on are all useful in developing an understanding of the setting or group studied.

Archival data are the routinely gathered records of a society, community, or organization, and may further supplement other qualitative methods. For example, marital patterns among a group of native Mexicans, discovered through fieldwork in a community, could be tested through marriage records found in the offices of the county seat or state capitol. Descriptions of articulated funding priorities by policy makers could be corroborated (or not) through an analysis of budgetary allocations. The decision to gather and analyze documents or archival records should be linked to the research questions developed in the conceptual framework of the study.

The use of documents often entails a specialized approach called *content analysis*. Best thought of as an overall approach, a method, *and* an analytic strategy, content analysis entails the systematic examination of forms of communication to document patterns objectively. A more objectivist approach than other qualitative methods, traditional content analysis allows the researcher to obtain an "objective and quantitative description" (Berelson, 1952, p. 18) of the content of various forms of communications. The raw material of content analysis may be any form of communication, usually written materials (textbooks, novels, newspapers); other forms of commu-

communication, however—such as music, pictures, or political speeches—may also be included.

Probably the greatest strengths of the content analysis method are that it is unobtrusive and nonreactive: It can be conducted without disturbing the setting in any way. The researcher determines where the greatest emphasis lies after the data have been gathered. Also, the method of procedure is explicit to the reader. Facts can therefore be checked, as can the care with which the analysis has been applied. For more about the use of content analysis in qualitative research, see Cohen and Fredler (1974), Funkhouser (1973), Gottschalk (1979), Greenberg (1980), and Luckenbill (1981).

Supplemental Data Collection Techniques

In addition to the primary data gathering methods outlined above, several supplemental methods can be incorporated in the design of a study, as appropriate. Each of these is a full and complete method in and of itself and has a methodological literature explicating its nuances and subtleties. As in the above discussions, the ones below are necessarily simplified and brief, and the list is not exhaustive. The methods discussed are narratives; life histories; historical analysis; film, video, and photography; kinesics; proxemics; unobtrusive measures; surveys and questionnaires; and projective techniques and psychological testing.

Narratives

In narrative inquiry, people's individual life stories are the focus. This method assumes that people live "storied lives" and seeks to collect data to describe those lives. As an interdisciplinary method, narratology draws from traditions in literary theory, oral history, drama, psychology, folklore, and film philosophy, and views lives holistically (Connelly & Clandinin, 1990). The researcher explores a story told by a participant and records that story through the construction of narrative. Narrative analysis can be applied to any spoken or written account; for example, an in-depth interview.

Narrative inquiry requires a great deal of sensitivity between participant and researcher: The inquiry should be a mutual and sincere collaboration, a caring relationship akin to friendship that is established over time for full participation in the storytelling, retelling, and reliving of personal experiences. It demands intense active listening and giving the narrator full voice. However, because it is a collaboration, both voices are heard.

This method is criticized for its focus on the individual rather than social context. Like life histories, however, it seeks to understand sociological questions about groups, communities, and contexts through the individual's lived experience. Like all data dependent on participants' accounts, narrative may suffer from selective recall, a focus on subsets of experience, filling in memory gaps through inference, and reinterpretation of the past (Ross & Conway, 1986). Crites (1986, p. 168) cautions against "the illusion of causality"—the inference that the narrator's story sequencing has accurate cause-and-effect linkages. Narrative inquiry is also time-consuming and laborious and requires some specialized training (Viney & Bousefield, 1991). A final disadvantage is its newness: It is difficult to identify standards and common definitions or criteria for good narrative inquiry.

Although narrative inquiry as a qualitative research method is relatively new, it has a long tradition in the humanities. Its strength is the elicitation of voice, with a lessening of the researcher's framework and interpretation. Narrative values the signs, symbols, and expression of feelings in language, validating how the narrator constructs meaning. It is particularly useful in developing feminist and critical theory (Eisner, 1988; Grumet, 1988).

Narrative inquiry may rely on journal records, photographs, letters, autobiographical writing, and other data. Typically, field notes are shared with the narrator, and the construction of the written record may be done collaboratively. In the conduct of narrative inquiry there is open recognition that the researcher is collaboratively constructing the narrator's reality, not just passively recording and reporting. Connelly and Clandinin (1990) assert that researchers need to "be prepared to follow their nose and, after the fact, reconstruct their narrative of inquiry" (p. 7). This becomes, in effect, the recounting of methodology. For more discussion of evolving issues in narrative inquiry, see Connelly and Clandinin (1990), Hollingsworth (1991), Mitchell (1981), Polkinghorne (1988), Sarbin (1986), Viney and Bousefield (1991), and Webb (1990).

Life Histories

The life history approach is used across the social science disciplines and is particularly useful for giving the reader an insider's view of a culture

(Edgerton & Langness, 1974). Dollard's (1935) classic work proposes a definition of the life history as a deliberate attempt to define the growth of a person in a cultural milieu and to make theoretical sense of it. Thus one understands a culture through the history of one person's development or life within it. Taylor and Bogdan (1984) describe the life history as a description of "the important events and experiences in a person's life," told in ways that capture "the person's own feelings, views, and perspectives" (p. 143). The life history is often an account of how a new person enters a group and becomes an adult capable of meeting the traditional expectations of that society for a person of that individual's gender and age. Life history studies emphasize the experiences and requirements of the individual—how the person copes with society, rather than how society copes with the stream of individuals (Mandelbaum, 1973).

Life histories are helpful in defining problems and in studying aspects of certain professions. Their value goes beyond the usefulness of providing specific information about events and customs of the past by showing how the individual interacts with the culture. Life histories are valuable in studying cultural changes that have occurred over time, in learning about cultural deviance, and in gaining an inside view of a culture. They also help capture the evolution of cultural patterns and how the patterns are linked to the life of an individual—their significance and the individual's reactions. Often this point of view is missing from standard ethnographies (Edgerton & Langness, 1974).

One strength of life history methodology is that, because it pictures the total course of a person's life, the reader enters vicariously into the same experiences. Second, the method provides a fertile source of hypotheses that may be tested by further study. Third, it indicates behavior processes and personality types that may be analyzed when a sufficient number of detailed life histories are accumulated for comparative study. Life history methodology emphasizes the value of a person's own story and provides pieces for a "mosaic" or total picture of a concept. Interconnections of apparently unconnected phenomena can be seen. Life histories are currently used a great deal in feminist research as a way of understanding, free of androcentric bias, how women's lives and careers evolve (Lawless, 1991).

The major limitations of the life history are its perceived lack of generality, the lack of accepted principles for the selection of participants, and a paucity of suitable analytical concepts to establish a coherent frame of reference. Once the researcher is cognizant of the possible weaknesses in the research methodology, he can circumvent them. Official records can be secured and the accounts of subjects checked against written reports. The researcher can corroborate the events presented in the history by interviewing others in the subject's life. Prior to publishing *The Professional Thief,* Sutherland and Conwell (1983) submitted the manuscript to four professional thieves and to two police detectives to correct for possible bias and to ensure that the data were accurate for professional thieves in general.

The abundance of data collected in a life history should be channeled in some preliminary way before analytic headway can be made (Dollard, 1935). Mandelbaum (1973) suggests three alternatives to chronological order as a way to organize and present the data: (1) the dimensions or aspects of the person's life; (2) the principal turnings and the life conditions between turnings; and (3) the person's characteristic means of adaptation.

Life histories have strong appeal to readers because of the subject matter and the narrative form in which they are written. A life history account adds much flavor to any qualitative study. For more on this subject, and some classical life history accounts, see Bogdan and Taylor (1975), Chessman (1954), Dollard (1935), Edgerton and Langness (1974), Keiser (1969), Mandelbaum (1973), Minister (1991), and Taylor and Bogdan (1984).

Historical Analysis

A history is an account of some past event or combination of events. Historical analysis is, therefore, a method of discovering, from records and accounts, what happened in the past. Historical analysis is particularly useful in qualitative studies for establishing a baseline or background prior to participant observation or interviewing.

Sources of historical data are classified as either primary or secondary. Primary sources include the oral testimony of eyewitnesses, documents, records, and relics. Secondary sources include the reports of persons who relate the accounts of actual eyewitnesses and summaries, as in history books and encyclopedias.

The researcher should consider various sources of historical data, such as contemporary records, including instructions, stenographic records, business and legal papers, and personal notes and memos; confidential reports, including military records, journals and diaries, and personal letters; public reports, including newspaper reports and memoirs or autobiographies; questionnaires; government documents, including archives and regulations;

opinions, including editorials, speeches, pamphlets, letters to the editor, and public opinion polls; fiction, songs, and poetry; and folklore.

Historical analysis is particularly useful in obtaining knowledge of previously unexamined areas and in reexamining questions for which answers are not as definite as desired. It allows for systematic and direct classification of data. Historical research traditions demand procedures to verify the accuracy of statements about the past, to establish relationships, and to determine the direction of cause-effect relationships. In fact, many research studies have a historical base or context, so systematic historical analysis enhances the trustworthiness and credibility of a study.

In historical analysis care must be taken to avoid the imposition of modern thought patterns on an earlier era, although this can be legitimately disputed. Sensitivity should be given to the interpretation of the statements of others. Historical analysis cannot use a direct observation approach and there is no way to test a historical hypothesis. There are also weaknesses in the classification of historical data. Documents may be falsified deliberately or may have been subject to incorrect interpretations on the part of the recorder. Words and phrases used in old records may now have different meanings. The meanings of relics are perceived and interpreted by the investigator. Errors in recording as well as frauds, hoaxes, and forgeries pose problems in dealing with the past. Thus the researcher should retain a modest skepticism about the data. For further reading on the use of historical analysis, see Barzun and Graff (1970), Brooks (1969), Fischer (1970), Gottschalk (1969), and Schatzman and Strauss (1973).

Films, Videos, and Photographs

Films and photographs have a long history in anthropology. Called *visual anthropology* or *film ethnography,* this tradition relies on films and photographs to capture the daily life of the group under study. Films provide visual records of passing natural events and may be used as permanent resources. The concept and method of the research film have emerged and are compatible with a variety of research methods, and have been used to describe how people navigate in public places (Ryave & Schenkein, 1974) and the use of space (Whyte, 1980), to present findings (Jackson, 1978), and to empower participants (Ziller & Lewis, 1981).

Research filming is a powerful tool for inquiry into past events. Film has the unique ability to capture visible phenomena seemingly objectively—

yet always from the perspective of the filmmaker. Research film methodology requires the documentation of the time, place, and subject of the filming, as well as the photographer's intent and interests. Also, a great wealth of visual information emanates from all natural events—to attempt a "complete" record of even a small event would be a fruitless pursuit.

There are three kinds of sampling in films: opportunity, programmed, and digressive (Sorenson, 1968). Opportunity sampling documents unanticipated or poorly understood phenomena as they occur. Programmed sampling involves filming according to a predetermined plan—deciding in advance what, where, and when to film. Grounded in the research proposal's conceptual framework, this sampling strategy stipulates which events are likely to be significant. Such filming is guided by the research design rather than by intuition, as in opportunity sampling. Digressive sampling is deliberate searching beyond the obvious to the novel, to the places and events that are usually outside typical public recognition.

Researchers choose to use ethnographic film for its obvious strengths. The visual samples increase the value of any record. It documents life crises and ceremonies, transmits cultural events to successive generations, and documents social conflicts (court, speakers, Senate sessions, and so on). The film researcher is limited only by what the mind can imagine and the camera can record. And, of course, events are documented in the natural setting.

Film is particularly valuable for discovery and validation. It documents nonverbal behavior and communication, such as facial expressions and emotions. Film preserves activity and change in original form. It can be used in the future to take advantage of new methods of seeing, analyzing, and understanding the process of change. Film is an aid to the researcher when the nature of what is sought is known but the elements of it cannot be discovered because of the limitations of the human eye. Film allows for the preservation and study of data from nonrecurring, disappearing, or rare events. With films, interpretation of information can be validated by another researcher. Feedback can be obtained on the authenticity of interpretation and it can be retaken to correct errors. Two excellent examples of ethnographic film are *Educating Peter* (Home Box Office Project Knowledge, 1992), the story of the experiences of a boy with severe cognitive challenges in a regular classroom, and *High School,* a depiction of life in a comprehensive high school in the early 1970s (Wiseman, 1969).

Film has certain weaknesses and limitations. There are always fundamental questions, such as: What is the nature of truth? Does the film manipulate reality? Concern exists about professional bias and the interests of the filmmaker. On the practical side, film is expensive and most research budgets are minimal. Production can be problematic. The researcher needs technical expertise. And filming can be very intrusive, affecting settings and events. Film cannot be published as a part of a book, journal, or dissertation. And finally, serious consideration must be given to the ethics of ethnographic filming. For further reading on the use of films and photography in qualitative research, see Asch (1970), Collier and Collier (1986), Gardner (1974), Hockings (1975), Rollwagen (1988), Taylor and Bogdan (1984), and Wiseman (1969).

Kinesics

Learning about society can be enhanced if we study not only what people say with their lips, but what their body movements reveal as well. The study of body motion and its accompanying messages is a technique known as kinesics. Specifically, kinesics is the study of body motion communication. The motion is analyzed systematically in a way that allows the researcher to see and measure significant patterns in the communication process.

Birdwhistell (1970) asserts that nonverbal body behaviors function like significant sounds that combine into single or relatively complex units, like words. Body movements ranging from a single nod to a series of hand and leg gestures can attach additional meaning to spoken words. All kinesics research rests upon the assumption that, without being aware of it, humans are engaged constantly in adjustments to the presence and activities of other persons. People modify and react verbally and nonverbally; their nonverbal behavior is influenced by culture, gender, age, and other factors associated with psychological and social development.

Birdwhistell labels four channels in the communicative process: vocal, visual, olfactory, and tactile. It is important for the researcher to be aware of these channels, as the interaction between researcher and subject consists of a steady flow of nonverbal communication clues. Behind the words are messages both parties are communicating. Armed with a knowledge of nonverbal clues, the researcher can monitor subjects' behaviors, discovering their attitudes and giving their actions additional meaning. Body language can express unconscious thoughts that may be essential for observers to decode if they are to analyze situations accurately. Measuring devices are available for researchers to use not only in gaining a further understanding of kinesics but also in learning how to interpret body movements.

In the interpretation of body language lies one of the weaknesses of kinesics. Novice "body readers" who have a "pop psych" understanding of the science of kinesics may make incorrect, perhaps damaging, interpretations of behavior. Related closely to this possibility of misinterpretation is the fact that the body language concept can be trivialized. For example, many studies focus on frequency counts of isolated units of behavior that alone convey little meaning. Knowing that a person blinked 100 times during a 15-minute interview is not significant unless the context of the situation is also apparent.

The strengths of kinesic analysis are that it provides a view into unconscious thoughts and provides a means for triangulation of verbal data. A researcher can be more confident about the accuracy of information provided by a subject if the speaker's body language is congruent with his words. Also, the researcher can monitor her own nonverbal behavior in order to clarify messages sent to the subject and to stay in touch with her own feelings during data collection. Finally, measuring instruments are available for the researcher to use.

Kinesic analysis is limited because body language is not universal, and researchers must be aware of cultural differences. There are some gestures that signal different meanings in different cultures; for example, in some countries, an up-and-down head nod signifies no and side-to-side movement of the head means yes. Body movements must be interpreted in context, and fine-tuned kinesic interpretations can be made only by experts. Body language such as movements of tiny jaw or neck muscles or amount of pupil dilation cannot be comprehended fully by a novice. The classical writings on kinesics are found in the work of Birdwhistell (1970); more current work includes that of Bull (1983) and Rutter (1984).

Proxemics

Proxemics is the study of people's use of space and its relationship to culture. The term was coined by Hall (1966), although he did not perform the original work in this area. Many studies have been conducted on the activities that take place in bars, airports, subways, and other public places where individuals have to deal with one another in limited space. Using proxemics, the researcher focuses on space, ranging from interpersonal distance to the arrangement of furniture and architecture. Anthropologists have used proxemics to determine the territorial customs of particular cultures. Proxemics have been useful in the study of the behavior of students in the classroom and of marital partners undergoing counseling.

There are several advantages to the use of proxemics. It is unobtrusive, and usually it is difficult for a subject to mislead the observer deliberately. Because proxemics is concerned with nonverbal behavior, subjects would have to be skillful in order to "lie" about their feelings. Proxemics is useful for studying the way individuals react to others regarding space and the invasion of their territory. Likewise, proxemics can be used in cross-cultural studies, because people's use of personal space varies greatly from one culture to the next. Finally, proxemic analysis is useful for studies in such areas as the effect of seating arrangements on student behavior or the effect of crowding on workplace productivity.

The greatest disadvantage of proxemics as a data collection method is that the researcher must be skilled in the interpretation of the observed behaviors in order to gain accurate information. If the researcher is observing a conference or a business meeting, the manner in which the subjects take their seats can be of vital importance, but the data must be interpreted carefully. Exclusive reliance on proxemics could be misleading, as it might suggest relationships that do not exist. Because of the relative youth of proxemics as a data collection method, there are few space measurement instruments available in the field of research, further limiting its diverse use.

The use of proxemics is increasing throughout research arenas. It provides a revealing and interesting method of gathering information about individual social behavior. For further reading on this subject, see Berman and Smith (1984), Crane and Griffin (1983), Edgerton (1979), Freedman (1975), Hall (1966), Hall and Hall (1977), Hinton (1985), Loughlin and Suina (1983), and Scheflen (1976).

Unobtrusive Measures

Unobtrusive measures are methods for collection of data that do not require the cooperation of the subjects and, in fact, may be "invisible" to them. Webb, Campbell, Schwartz, and Sechrest (1966) describe these measures as "nonreactive research," because the researcher is expected to observe or gather data without interfering in the ongoing flow of everyday events. Data collected in this manner are categorized as documents, archival records, and physical evidence. Of the three, documents and archival records are the most frequently used in qualitative studies and were discussed above.

Physical evidence not produced specifically for the purpose of research often constitutes data; the following example provides an illustration. During the 1960s, the floor tile around the hatching-chick exhibit at the Chicago Museum of Science and Industry had to be replaced every 6 weeks. The tile in other parts of the museum did not require replacement for years. The selective erosion of the tiles, indexed by the replacement rate, provided a measure of the relative popularity of exhibits (Webb et al., 1966).

Unobtrusive measures are particularly useful for triangulation. As a supplement to interviews, nonreactive research provides another perspective on the phenomenon, elaborating its complexity. These methods can be used without arousing notice from subjects, and data collection is relatively easy because it often involves using data (e.g., bills, archival records, sales records) already collected by someone else.

When used in isolation, however, unobtrusive measures may distort the picture. Erosion and survival may be affected by activities unknown to the researcher. For example, tiles near the hatching-chick exhibit may wear out because the exhibit is close to the candy machine, not because of the exhibit's popularity. Some researchers consider the use of unobtrusive methods to be unethical: They feel that those studied should be informed of the nature of the research.

When the researcher needs information on measures of frequency or attendance, when direct observation would be impossible or would bias the data, this method is useful. Unobtrusive data collection is often aided by hardware such as audiotapes, hidden cameras, one-way mirrors, gauges, and infrared photos. Determined researchers might even search through garbage for insights into behavior, as some journalists have. For additional information about the use of unobtrusive measures, see Christensen (1960), Maddock, Kenny, Lupfer, and Rosen (1977), Sechrest (1979), Webb and Weick (1979), and Webb et al. (1966).

Questionnaires and Surveys

Researchers administer questionnaires to some sample of a population to learn about the distribution of characteristics, attitudes, or beliefs. In deciding to survey the group of people chosen for study, researchers make one critical assumption—that the characteristic or belief can be described or measured accurately through self-report. In using questionnaires, researchers rely totally on the honesty and accuracy of participants' responses. Although this limits the usefulness of questionnaires in delving into tacit beliefs and deeply held values, there are still many occasions when surveying the group under study can be useful.

Questionnaires typically entail several questions that have structured response categories and may include some that are open-ended. The questions are examined (sometimes quite vigorously) for bias, sequence, clarity, and face validity. Questionnaires usually are tested through administration to small groups to determine their usefulness and, perhaps, reliability.

Sample surveys consist of the collection of data in a standardized format, usually from a probability sample of the population. The survey is the preferred method if the researcher wishes to obtain a small amount of information from a large number of subjects.

Survey research is the appropriate mode of inquiry for making inferences about a large group of people from data drawn on a relatively small number of individuals from that group. The basic aim of survey research is to describe and explain statistically the variability of certain features of a population. The general logic of survey research gives a distinctive style to the research process; the type of survey instrument is determined by the information needed. There are three types of surveys: mail, telephone, and personal interview. Any method of data collection, however, from observation to content analysis, can be and has been used in survey research.

Most survey studies involve cross-sectional measurements made at a single point in time, or longitudinal measurements taken at several different times. Other forms of survey research include trend studies examining a population by studying separate samples at different points in time, cohort studies examining a bounded population, and panel studies examining a single sample of individuals at several points in time. Analysis of survey data takes the form of quantitative analysis that relies mainly on either descriptive or inferential statistics.

The relative advantages and disadvantages of survey research are highlighted through the following criteria: (1) appropriateness of the method to the problem studied, (2) accuracy of measurement, (3) generalizability of the findings, (4) administrative convenience, and (5) avoidance of ethical or political difficulties in the research process.

There are some definite advantages of surveys when the goals of research require obtaining quantitative data on a certain problem or population. Surveys facilitate research in politically or ethically sensitive areas. They are used in programs for public welfare or economic development. Large surveys often focus on sensitive or controversial topics within the public domain.

Strengths of surveys include their accuracy, generalizability, and convenience. Accuracy in measurement is enhanced by quantification, replicability, and control over observer effects. Survey results can be generalized to a larger population within known limits of error. Surveys are amenable to rapid statistical analysis and are comparatively easy to administer and manage.

Surveys have weaknesses, however. For example, they are of little value for examining complex social relationships or intricate patterns of interaction. The strengths of surveys can also be weaknesses. Although controlling accuracy, a survey cannot assure without further evidence that the sample represents a broader universe. Thus the method of drawing the sample and the sample size is critical to the accuracy of the study and its potential for generalizability. Also, even though surveys are convenient, they are generally a relatively expensive method of data collection. Finally, surveys may result in an invasion of privacy or produce questionable effects in the respondent or the community. Some research projects may enhance the position or resources of a particular group, and conflicts frequently arise between sponsors and research teams concerning how problems are defined. For further reading on the use of survey methods, see Alwin (1978), Belson (1982), Benson and Benson (1975), Jick (1979), and Sudman and Bradburn (1982).

Projective Techniques and Psychological Testing

Some types of interpretive psychological strategies were developed many years ago by clinical psychologists to obtain personality data. These strategies have been used fairly extensively in comparative studies about culture and for analysis of personality dynamics. Based on an internal, perceptual frame of reference, the techniques assume that one can get a valid picture of a person by assessing the way the individual projects his or her personality onto some standard, ambiguous stimuli.

Standardization and ambiguity are common elements in tests of this nature, although "clinical" judgments are the primary interpretation bases of responses to these stimuli. Results are typically expressed in the form of a verbal report assessing the subject's dominant needs and ambitions, tolerance of frustrations, attitudes toward authority, major internal conflicts, and so on. The reputation and qualifications of the tester sometimes play a role in how the report is received and how much credibility is attached to the interpretation.

Two of the most well-known and frequently used psychological strategies of this notion are the Rorschach inkblot test and the Thematic Apperception Test (TAT). The original ideas behind both included the assumption that the stimuli should be ambiguous so that the subject would have to be imaginative and "projective" in response to the situation.

The Rorschach test utilizes pictures (symmetrical inkblots) that are usually presented in a predetermined order, with the subject reporting what each picture resembles or suggests. The number, quality, and variety of the subject's responses are compared against specific personality types and against prior experiences with the responses of other people to the same stimuli. In the Thematic Apperception Test, the subject is asked to tell stories about a set of picture scenes. Test results are used to assess personality traits such as aggressiveness, dependence, and sexual conflicts.

Although projective instruments have been the object of considerable criticism for many years, they are still commonly employed in clinical contexts by psychologists. Yet, questions remain as to their validity and reliability; environmental and cultural factors may also affect results. Today, concern focuses on more concrete aspects of personality traits, such as self-esteem and styles of interpersonal behavior, rather than the vague generalizations that characterized earlier interpretive schemes.

Recently a number of other psychological tests and measurements have been developed for use in qualitative and anthropological research. Examples include the study of (1) the perception of illusions, which uses optical and auditory illusions to examine differences in perception related to differences in types of environments; (2) judgments of aesthetic qualities, which rely on pictures of art objects or musical stimuli to elicit opinions concerning aesthetic excellence; (3) psychomotor skills, which use physical activity measures to indicate personality qualities such as introversion and extroversion; (4) games people play, to provide significant information about community and social behavior; and (5) games as a laboratory device, which uses a specific game involving family members to determine a relationship between communication patterns and socioeconomic differences.

Various other qualitative methods have been devised for studying entire communities, group living patterns, and social integration of individuals in different residential contexts. Rizzutto's *The Birth of a Living God* (1979), and Coles's *Children of Crisis: Vol. 2, Migrants, Sharecroppers, Mountaineers* (1971) and *Privileged Ones: The Well-Off and the Rich in America* (1977) are good examples of the use of projective techniques in a qualitative mode. For further reading on this topic, see Naroll and Cohen (1970) and Pelto and Pelto (1978).

Combining Data Collection Methods

Many qualitative studies combine several data collection methods over the course of the study. The researcher can assess the strengths and limitations of each method, then decide if that method will work with the particular questions and in the particular setting for a given study. Tables 4.1 and 4.2 display the strengths and limitations of each data collection method, based on how it is generally used in qualitative studies. The tables should help researchers to select the best combination of methods: Limitations in one method can be compensated for by the strengths of a complementary one.

In drafting the proposal, the researcher should consider whether the method will provide adequate information, be cost effective, and be feasible in terms of the sensitivities in the setting and the resources available for the study. The relative emphasis on participation in many qualitative studies, for example, suggests certain methods over others. Lutz and Iannaccone (1969) provide guidelines for method selection based on role, as shown in Table 4.3. These choices should be logically linked to the conceptual framework and research questions, the overall strategy of the study, and early decisions about role.

Vignette 19 describes how a researcher selected specific data collection methods to elicit information about a long-term health care facility.

Vignette 19

Choosing Data Collection Methods

How might one's view of life be shaped by residence in a long-term health care facility? Having posed that question, a doctoral student in health care management decided that qualitative research methods would provide the most appropriate approach to her research. Contexts,

Table 4.1 Strengths of Data Collection Methods

Strengths	PO	I	EGI	ELI	FGI	DR	N	LH	HA	F	Q	P	K	PT	UM
Data easy to manipulate and categorize for data analysis	.	.	.	.	.	x	.	.	.	.	x	x	x	.	D
Face-to-face encounter with informants	x	x	x	x	x	.	x	x	.	.	.	.	.	D	.
Obtains large amounts of expansive and contextual data quickly	x	x	.	x	x	.	x	x	x	x	.	.	.	x	.
Facilitates cooperation from research subject	x	x	x	x	x	.	D	x	x	x	.	.	.	.	.
Facilitates access for immediate follow-up data collection for clarification and omissions	x	x	x	.	x	x	x	x	x	x	.	D	D	.	x
Allows wide range of types of data and informants, thus avoiding sampling of "pocket of the universe"	x	.	.	.	D	.	.	.	.	.	.	D	D	.	x
Easy and efficient to administer and manage	.	.	.	.	.	x	.	.	x	.	x	x	x	x	x
Easily quantifiable and amenable to statistical analysis	.	.	.	.	.	x	.	.	.	.	x	x	x	x	x
Useful for discovering complex interconnections in social relationships	x	x	x	x	x	.	x	x	.	x	.	x	x	.	.
Easy to establish generalizability	x	x	x	x	D	x	x	x	x	.	x	x	x	D	.
Data are collected in natural setting	x	x	x	x	D	x	x	x	x	x	x	x	.	x	.
Good for documenting major events, crises, social conflicts	.	.	.	x	x	x	x	x	x	x	x	x	.	.	x
Good for obtaining data on nonverbal behavior and communication	x	.	D	.	x	.	D	.	.	x	.	x	x	D	x
Collects data on unconscious thoughts and behavior	x	.	.	.	x	x	D	.	.	x	.	x	x	x	x
Previous researchers have developed usable measuring devices	.	.	.	.	.	x	.	.	.	x	x	x	x	x	x
Facilitates analysis, validity checks, and triangulation	x	x	x	x	D	x	.	x	x	x	x	x	x	x	x
Facilitates discovery of nuances in culture	x	x	x	x	D	x	x	x	x	x	x	x	.	.	x
Provides for flexibility in the formulation of hypotheses	x	x	x	x	x	D	x	x	x	x	.	.	x	.	x
Provides background context for more focus on activities, behaviors, and events	x	x	.	x	x	.	x	x	x	x	.	.	x	.	.
Great utility for uncovering the subjective side, the "native's perspective" of organizational processes	x	x	x	x	D	.	x	x	x	x	.	x	x	.	.

NOTE: x = strength exists; D = depends on use. PO = Participant Observation, I = Interview, EGI = Ethnographic Interviewing, ELI = Elite Interviewing, FGI = Focus Group Interviewing, DR = Document Review, N = Narratives, LH = Life History, HA = Historical Analysis, F = Film, Q = Questionnaire, P = Proxemics, K = Kinesics, PT = Psychological Techniques, UM = Unobtrusive Measures.

Table 4.2 Weaknesses of Data Collection Methods

Weaknesses	PO	I	EGI	ELI	FGI	DR	N	LH	HA	F	Q	P	K	PT	UM
Can lead the researcher to "miss the forest while observing the trees"	x	·	x	·	D	x	x	x	·	x	x	x	x	x	x
Data are open to misinterpretation due to cultural differences	x	x	·	x	x	x	x	x	·	x	x	·	·	x	x
Requires specialized technical training for data collection	·	·	x	·	x	·	·	·	·	x	x	x	x	x	·
Dependent upon the cooperation of a small group of key informants	x	x	x	x	·	·	x	x	·	·	·	·	·	·	x
Fraught with ethical dilemmas	x	·	·	x	·	·	x	x	·	x	x	·	·	x	x
Difficult to replicate; procedures are not always explicit or are dependent upon researcher's opportunity or characteristics	x	x	x	x	x	·	x	x	·	x	·	·	·	·	·
Data often subject to observer effects; obtrusive and reactive	x	x	x	x	x	·	x	x	·	x	x	·	x	·	x
Expensive materials and equipment	·	·	x	·	·	·	·	·	·	x	·	·	x	x	·
Can cause danger or discomfort for researcher	·	x	·	x	x	·	·	·	x	·	·	·	·	x	·
Especially dependent upon the honesty of those providing the data	x	x	x	x	D	·	x	x	·	·	x	x	x	x	·
An overly artistic or literary style of presentation can obscure the research	·	·	·	·	·	x	·	·	·	·	·	·	·	·	·
Highly dependent on the "goodness" of the initial research question	·	·	·	·	·	·	x	·	D	x	x	x	x	x	x
Highly dependent upon the ability of the researchers to be resourceful, systematic, and honest, to control bias	x	x	x	x	x	·	x	x	x	x	·	·	·	·	x

NOTE: x = weakness exists; D = depends on use. PO = Participant Observation, I = Interview, EGI = Ethnographic Interviewing, ELI = Elite Interviewing, FGI = Focus Group Interviewing, DR = Document Review, N = Narratives, LH = Life History, HA = Historical Analysis, F = Film, Q = Questionnaire, P = Proxemics, K = Kinesics, PT = Psychological Techniques, UM = Unobtrusive Measures.

Table 4.3   Data Collection Methods Related to Observation Role

Methods Useful in Data Collection	I Participant as an Observer	II Observer as a Participant	III Observer as a Non-participant	Comment
		Roles		
1. Observation and recording of descriptive data	+	+	+	particularly useful to Role I in areas of guarded interaction and sentiment
2. Recording direct quotes of sentiment	+	+	*	same as above
3. Unstructured interview	+	+	*	if the researcher is skillful, a structure emerges
4. Structured interview guides	−	*	+	most useful in survey work (e.g., census)
5. Detailed interaction tally guides (e.g., Flanders and Bales Interaction guides)	−	−	*	most useful in small-group work
6. Interaction frequency tallies	+	+	+	meaningful in leadership studies
7. Paper and pencil tests questionnaires				very helpful in certain circumstances for
scales	−	−	+	certain purposes
achievement or	−	−	+	
ability	−	−	*	
8. Written records				very important to Role I in
newspaper	+	+	*	checking reliability of
official minutes	+	+	*	observed data
letters	+	+	*	
speeches	+	+	*	
9. Radio and television reports	+	+	*	same as above

SOURCE: Lutz & Iannaccone (1969, p. 113). Reprinted by permission.
NOTE: + = likely to be used; * = may occasionally be used; − = difficult or impossible to use.

processes, and interactions would require examination, therefore a qualitative approach, affirmed by Glaser and Strauss (1967) as offering "sensitivity in picking up everyday facts about social structures social systems" (p. 15), seemed the most logical.

The researcher (Kalnins, 1986) needed to understand the meanings given to events by participants. She referred to the work of Schatzman and Strauss (1973) by noting that:

The researcher *must* get close to the people whom he studies; he [sic] understands that their actions are best comprehended when observed on the spot—in the natural, ongoing environment where they live and work.... The researcher himself [sic] must be at the location, not only to watch but also to listen to the symbolic sounds that characterize this world. A dialogue with persons in their natural situations will reveal the nuances of meaning from which their perspectives and definitions are continually forged. (Kalnins, 1986, pp. 5-6)

From the variety of data collection strategies, she proposed a combination of direct observation, participant observation, and semistructured interviewing. Her beginning point would be direct observation of residents and staff in various areas of the facility, "witnessing events which particularly preoccupy the hosts, or indicate special symbolic importance to them" (Schatzman & Strauss, 1973, p. 59). This would allow her to get a holistic view and to gather data that would inform the structuring of the interview process.

Kalnins's plan as participant observer would be to observe the residents and staff in the natural setting of the long-term health care facility, requiring her "commitment to adopt the perspective of those studied by sharing in their day-to-day experiences" (Denzin, 1970, p. 185). Participant observation is actually a blending of various techniques, a "style or strategy of research, a characteristic type of research which makes use of several methods and techniques organized in a distinctive research design" (McCall & Simmons, 1969, p. 341).

In the proposal, Kalnins anticipated that participant observation and interviewing would run concurrently, allowing data from each to be used to substantiate events, test emerging hypotheses, and make further decisions about the conduct of the research. As Becker and Geer (1969) point out, participant observation allows the researcher to (1) check definitions of terms the participants use in the interview in a more natural setting (i.e., casual conversations with others); (2) observe events the participants cannot report because "they do not want to, feeling that to speak of some particular subject would be impolitic, impolite, or insensitive" (p. 326); and (3) observe situations described in interviews and thus become aware of distortions presented by the participants.

Her role as participant observer would mean Kalnins would become immersed in the lives and activities of those being studied. She understood the interactive-adaptive nature of participant observation, reflecting the complex relationship between field observation and emerging theory, and the impact of this relationship on decisions about further data collection. Decisions about the data to be collected and methods for collecting those data were guided by Wilson's (1977, p. 255) list of five relevant types of data employed to get at meaning structures: (1) the form and content of verbal interaction between participants, (2) the form and content of verbal interaction with researcher, (3) nonverbal behavior, (4) patterns of actions and nonaction, and (5) traces, archival records, artifacts, and documents.

In order to generate facts, opinions, and insights (Yin, 1984), Kalnins planned for open-ended structured interviews (using questionnaires) that would enable the exploration of many topics but could focus on cultural nuances, firsthand encounters, and the perceptions, meanings, and interpretations of others. Information would also be gathered from various documents and archives, lending a historical perspective to the study.

Vignette 19 illustrates how a researcher chose an array of data collection methods, knowing that each method had particular strengths and how each would help elicit certain desired information. One advantage of using multiple qualitative methods is the potential to evoke unexpected data. Having decided to pursue qualitative research, the student above was prepared to adapt procedures if necessitated by changes in the field. This vignette shows that data collection strategies and methods cannot be chosen in a vacuum. Intensive examination of the possible methods, trying them out, examining their potentials, and fitting them to the research question, site, and sample are important design considerations. In addition, researchers must consider their *own* personal abilities in carrying out any particular overall approach or method.

General Principles for Designing Data Collection Strategies

In the proposal, the methods planned for data collection should be related to the type of information sought. Zelditch's (1962) chart, reproduced in Table 4.4, provides guidelines for three large categories of methods: enumerating, participant observation, and in-depth interviewing.

Table 4.4   Information Types and Methods of Obtaining Information

Information Types	Methods of Obtaining Information		
	Enumerations and Samples	Participant Observation	Interviewing Informants
Frequency distributions	prototype and best form	usually inadequate and inefficient	often, but not always, inadequate; if adequate, efficient
Incidents, histories	not adequate by itself; not efficient	prototype and best form	adequate, with precautions, and efficient
Institutionalized norms and statuses	adequate, but inefficient	adequate, but inefficient, except for unverbalized norms	most efficient and hence best form

SOURCE: Zelditch (1962, p. 575). Reprinted by permission.

Each broad category best yields a particular type of information. In determining which method to use, the researcher should carefully examine the questions guiding the study: Many questions that appear to be "how" questions are really "how many" questions in disguise. For example, the selection of participant observation to help uncover how a program developed will not adequately respond to the "how many" questions that might be embedded in it.

The researcher should determine the most practical, efficient, feasible, and ethical methods for collecting data as the research progresses. He might start with participant observation as he seeks to identify questions, patterns, and domains. This strategy may change as the research becomes more focused and progresses toward more specific questions and clearer concepts that suggest the use of representative samples. Then the researcher could develop surveys and enumerate the findings. On the other hand, the findings might be descriptions, not numbers. If the research goal is description of processes, concepts, categories, and typologies, then sampling and counting are merely tools of analysis, not necessarily part of the research findings. The proposal should demonstrate that the researcher is capable of designing and selecting data collection methods that are appropriate, well thought out, and thorough. Because the research question may change as the research progresses, the methods may change and the researcher must ensure this flexibility. Vignette 20 provides an example.

Vignette 20
_____

Design Flexibility [2]

A study is proposed that will explore the implementation of a mandate for local school councils. The researcher first proposes participant observation of meetings and in-depth interviews with board members. The data collection plan shows a schedule for observing the meetings, goals for interviewing, and a time allowance for analysis of data and for follow-up data collection. But, in the process of initial data collection and preliminary analysis, the researcher discovers that teacher resentment of the councils is creating a pattern of unintended negative consequences. This discovery could have important implications for policy development. Must the researcher stick with the original question and data collection plan? Wouldn't a design alteration offer important insights?

If the researcher could describe the processes whereby well-intended policy is thwarted, policy makers could gain insight that might help them make timely alterations in policy development or implementation. Given this possible benefit to the study, the researcher might then choose to focus subsequent data collection on the conflicts between teacher needs and the mandate to school boards that they implement councils. This would require the researcher to turn to additional literatures on, for example, teacher needs, teacher participation in decision making, or teacher unions. The researcher might also need to employ additional data collection methods (such as surveying teacher needs, observing teacher union meetings, and historical research on the reactions of teacher lobbies to mandates for school councils) or to sample additional settings or people. As the research question became more focused, the research design and data collection strategy would most likely undergo some changes.

In the example in Vignette 20, the research proposal probably did not include a plan for analysis of lobbying efforts or observation of collective bargaining sessions. It would be entirely appropriate, however, indeed recommended, for the researcher to modify the research proposal if an exciting and significant focus emerges from early data collection. In fact, the primary strength of the qualitative approach is this very flexibility that allows, even encourages, exploration, discovery, and creativity.

The next chapter addresses the complex processes of managing, recording, and analyzing data. Rather than discrete, sequential events, these processes occur iteratively throughout the conduct of a qualitative study: Analysis occurs as themes are identified, as the deeper structures of the social setting become clear, and as consequent modifications are made in the initial design. At the proposal stage, however, the researcher should present some initial ideas about how the data will be managed and stored, and provide some preliminary discussion of the processes of analyzing those data. These are discussed next.

5

Recording, Managing, and Analyzing Data

Once the overall strategy, site and sample selection, and data collection methods have been determined, the researcher should discuss how these voluminous data will be recorded, managed, and analyzed. At the proposal stage, this discussion can be brief but should provide the reader with a sense that the data will be recorded efficiently and managed in ways that allow for easy retrieval. In addition, initial strategies for analysis should be presented.

Recording and Managing Data

The proposal section on research design should include plans for recording data in a systematic manner that is appropriate and will facilitate analysis. If the proposal is more "objectivist" in assumptions, the researcher should demonstrate an awareness that techniques for recording observations, interactions, and interviews will not excessively intrude in the ongoing flow of daily events. In some situations, even note-taking interferes with, inhibits, or in some way acts upon the setting and the participants. Plans to use tape recorders, cameras, and other mechanical devices should be delineated in the proposal, demonstrating that the researcher will use data recording strategies that fit the setting and the participants' sensitivities, and that these will only be used with participants' consent.

In action and participatory research approaches, the researcher's intrusiveness in the setting is not an issue. Because these approaches are fundamentally interactive and include participants quite fully in framing questions and gathering data, the researcher's presence is considered a quite integral part of the setting. Whatever the qualitative approach, however, researchers should practice and build habits for labeling audiotapes, carrying extra batteries, and finding quiet places for note-taking; such practices will pay off by keeping data intact, complete, organized, and accessible.

In addition, the researcher should plan a system to ease retrieval for analysis. Planning ahead for color-coding notes to keep track of dates, names, titles, attendance at events, chronologies, descriptions of settings, maps, sociograms, and so on is invaluable for piecing together patterns, defining categories for data analysis, planning further data collection, and especially for writing the final product of the research. Vignette 21 provides descriptive detail of one such effort.

Vignette 21
_____

Data Management

In her dissertation research on women's socialization in school administration, Marshall (1979) developed a process by which data transcription, organization, and analysis were combined in a single operation. Her entry into the field and interviewing were directed by a conceptual framework and a set of guiding hypotheses.

Data analysis was conducted by trying out conceptual levers such as Goode's (1960) role strain theory, identified in the course of the literature review. Goode's theory guided the analysis of data pertaining to conflicts experienced by women entering male sex-typed careers while continuing to live with stereotypical expectations of mother, wife, and community member. Building upon Goode's work, Marshall devised a career-role strain theory that included feminine identity and sexuality crises prompted by the demands of working in a male-normed profession.

Employing constant comparative data analysis, she developed a grounded theory of women's socialization in male sex-typed careers that explained the socialization period of transition. During this period, women resist the pull of aspiration, resent the exclusion, are angry at the double demands, and yet simultaneously create new ways to fill the roles. Observational notes and pre-fieldwork mapping of sites or subjects were recorded on legal-sized, hard-backed notebooks that could be held in the lap or used on the run. Following each interview, Marshall added semitranscribed field notes of audiotaped conversations, selecting conceptually intriguing phrases that either connected with previous literature or suggested patterns emerging from the analysis of previous data.

The process of preserving the data and meanings on tape and the combined transcription and preliminary analysis greatly increased the efficiency of data analysis. The researcher's transcription, done with the literature review, previous data, and earlier analytic memos in mind, became a useful part of data analysis and not mere clerical duty.

This is not to suggest a reprieve from the transfer of data to index cards, coding of data, sorting of cards to identify overlapping categories, organization of codes into more inclusive and abstract domains, methodological notes, analytic memos, theoretical notes, case summaries, charts, and dummy tables, all representing further steps in analysis. Combining the initial transcription with analysis, however, moved the study forward efficiently and did so without threat to the exploratory value of qualitative research or to data quality.

Vignette 21 is just one researcher's way of managing complex and thick data. Over the years, researchers have developed a variety of data management strategies ranging from color and number codings on index cards to computer programs; these techniques are often shared as part of the "folklore of fieldwork." In addition, Schatzman and Strauss's (1973) suggestions on observational notes, methodological notes, theoretical notes, and analytic memos are quite useful. Whatever method is devised, it must enable the researcher to organize data while making them easily retrievable and manipulable.

Data Analysis Strategies

Data analysis is the process of bringing order, structure, and meaning to the mass of collected data. It is a messy, ambiguous, time-consuming, creative, and fascinating process. It does not proceed in a linear fashion; it is not neat. Qualitative data analysis is a search for general statements about relationships among categories of data; it builds grounded theory. Useful discussions and procedures are provided in Miles and Huberman (1993) and Patton (1990).

This section of the research proposal should describe to the reader initial decisions about data analysis and should convince the reader that the researcher is sufficiently knowledgeable about qualitative analysis to consider data organization, theme development and testing, and report writing. Although none of these can be given exhaustive consideration in the proposal, the researcher should convince the reader that thought and awareness have gone into planning the analysis phase of the study. What follows is a discussion of some considerations the researcher should bring to this section.

Whether the researcher structures some of the analysis before data collection or begins the process during data collection is a judgment call. Generating categories of data to collect, or cells in a matrix, can be an important focusing device for the study. Tightly structured, highly organized data gathering and analyzing schemes, however, often filter out the unusual, the serendipitous—the puzzle that if attended to and pursued, would provide a recasting of the entire research endeavor. Thus a balance must be struck between efficiency considerations and design flexibility.

In qualitative studies, data collection and analysis go hand in hand to promote the emergence of substantive theory grounded in empirical data. Glaser and Strauss (1967) and Vidich (1969) expand on this process. The researcher is guided by initial concepts and guiding hypotheses, but shifts or discards them as the data are collected and analyzed. Schatzman and Strauss (1973) succinctly portray the process of qualitative data collection and analysis:

> Qualitative data are exceedingly complex, and not readily convertible into standard measurable units of objects seen and heard; they vary in level of abstraction, in frequency of occurrence, in relevance to central questions in the research. Also, they vary in the source or ground from which they are experienced. . . . Our model researcher starts analyzing very early in the research process. For him, the option represents an *analytic* strategy: he needs to analyze as he goes along both to adjust his observation strategies, shifting some emphasis towards those experiences which bear upon the development of his understanding, and generally, to exercise control over his emerging ideas by virtually simultaneous "checking" or "testing" of these ideas. . . . Probably the most fundamental operation in the analysis of qualitative data is that of discovering significant *classes* of things, persons and events and the *properties* which characterize them. In this process, which continues throughout the research, the analyst gradually comes to reveal his own "is's" and "because's": he names classes and links one with another, at first with "simple" statements (propositions) that express the linkages, and continues this process until his propositions fall into *sets,* in an ever-increasing density of linkages. (pp. 108-110, emphasis in original)

The researcher should use the guiding hypotheses and the related literature developed earlier in the proposal. This earlier grounding and planning can be used to suggest several categories that can serve to code the data initially for subsequent analysis.

As theory with related concepts emerges from analysis, negative instances will lead to new data collecting and analysis that serve to strengthen theory. Theory solidifies as major modifications occur less often and concepts fall into established categories. Finally, analysis will be complete when the critical categories are defined, the relationships among them are established, and they are integrated into a grounded theory.

Analytic Procedures

Analytic procedures fall into five modes: organizing the data; generating categories, themes, and patterns; testing the emergent hypotheses against the data; searching for alternative explanations of the data; and writing the report. Each phase of data analysis entails *data reduction* as the reams of collected data are brought into manageable chunks, and *interpretation* as the researcher brings meaning and insight to the words and acts of the participants in the study.

The interpretive act remains mysterious in both qualitative and quantitative data analysis. It is a process of bringing meaning to raw, inexpressive data that is necessary whether the researcher's language is ANOVAs and means or rich description of ordinary events. Raw data have no inherent meaning; the interpretive act brings meaning to those data and displays that meaning to the reader through the written report.

Organizing the Data. Reading, reading, and reading once more through the data forces the researcher to become familiar with those data in intimate ways. People, events, and quotes sift constantly through the researcher's mind. During the reading process, the researcher can list on note cards the data available, perform the minor editing necessary to make field notes retrievable, and generally "clean up" (Pearsol, 1985) what seems overwhelming and unmanageable. At this time, the researcher could also enter the data into one of several software programs for the management and/or analysis of qualitative data (see Tesch, 1990, for an extended treatment of software for qualitative data analysis). As Patton (1980) notes:

> The data generated by qualitative methods are voluminous. I have found no way of preparing students for the sheer massive volumes of information with which they will find themselves confronted when data collection has ended. Sitting down to make sense out of pages of interviews and whole files of field notes can be overwhelming. (p. 297)

He then underscores how much of qualitative reporting consists of descriptive data, the purpose of which is to display the daily events of the phenomenon under study. Careful attention to how data are being reduced is necessary throughout the research endeavor. In some instances, direct transfer onto predeveloped data recording charts is most appropriate. Miles and Huberman (1993) suggest several schemata for recording qualitative data. Such techniques streamline data management, help ensure reliability across several researchers, and are highly recommended. In using graphics and schema, however, the researcher should guard against losing the serendipitous finding.

Generating Categories, Themes, and Patterns. The category generation phase of data analysis is the most difficult, complex, ambiguous, creative, and fun. Though there are few descriptions of this process in the literature, it remains the most amenable to display through example. The analytic process demands a heightened awareness of the data, a focused attention to those data, and an openness to the subtle, tacit undercurrents of social life. Identifying salient themes, recurring ideas or language, and patterns of belief that link people and settings together is the most intellectually challenging phase of data analysis and one that can integrate the entire endeavor. Through questioning the data and reflecting on the conceptual framework, the researcher engages the ideas and the data in significant intellectual work.

The process of category generation involves noting regularities in the setting or people chosen for study. As categories of meaning emerge, the researcher searches for those that have internal convergence and external divergence (Guba, 1978). That is, the categories should be internally consistent but distinct from one another. Here the researcher does not search for the exhaustive and mutually exclusive categories of the statistician, but instead to identify the salient, grounded categories of meaning held by participants in the setting.

Patton (1990) describes the processes of inductive analysis where the salient categories emerge from the data. The researcher may use "indigenous typologies" (p. 306) or "analyst-constructed typologies" (pp. 393-400) to reflect a classification scheme used by the people in the setting under study. Indigenous typologies are those created and expressed by participants and are generated through analyses of the local use of language.

Analyst-constructed typologies are those created by the researcher as reflecting distinct categories but not generative of separate language categories. In this case, the researcher applies a typology to naturally occurring

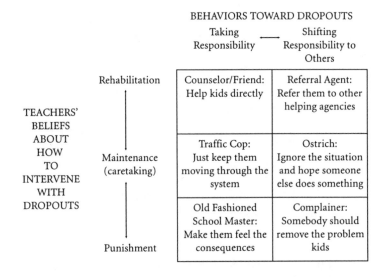

Figure 5.1. An Empirical Typology of Teacher Roles With High School Dropouts
SOURCE: Patton (1980, p. 315).

variations in observations. This process entails uncovering patterns, themes, and categories, and may well be subject to the "legitimate charge of imposing a world of meaning on the participants that better reflects the observer's world than the world under study" (Patton, 1990, p. 398). In a related strategy, through logical reasoning, classification schemes are crossed with one another to generate new insights or typologies for further exploration in the data. Usually presented in matrix format, these cross-classifications suggest "holes" in the already-analyzed data, suggesting areas where data might be *logically* uncovered. Patton (1990), however, cautions the researcher not to allow these matrices to lead the analysis but instead to generate sensitizing concepts to guide further explorations: "It is easy for a matrix to begin to manipulate the data as the analyst is tempted to force the data into categories created by the cross-classification to fill out the matrix and make it work" (p. 412). Examples of two logically constructed matrices are presented in Figures 5.1 and 5.2.

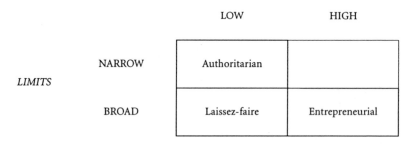

Figure 5.2. Three Ideal-Typical Approaches to Training and Dissemination
SOURCE: Firestone & Rossman (1986, p. 308)

Testing Emergent Hypotheses. As categories and patterns between them become apparent, the researcher begins the process of evaluating the plausibility of these developing hypotheses and testing them through the data. This entails a search through the data during which one challenges the hypotheses, searches for negative instances of the patterns, and incorporates these into larger constructs, if necessary.

Part of this phase is to evaluate the data for their informational adequacy, credibility, usefulness, and centrality. Although rigorous procedures can be set up to determine if, in fact, an informant is consistently truthful, a more reasonable stance is to approach the data with some skepticism and willingness to consider that the participants in the study have ensured a particular presentation of themselves (Goffman, 1959) to the researcher. Secondarily, the researcher must determine whether or not the data are useful in illuminating the questions being explored and whether or not they are central to the story that is unfolding about the social phenomenon.

Searching for Alternative Explanations. As categories and patterns between them emerge in the data, the researcher must engage in the critical act of challenging the very pattern that seems so apparent. The researcher must search for other, plausible explanations for these data and the linkages among them. Alternative explanations *always* exist; the researcher must search for, identify, and describe them, and then demonstrate how the explanation offered is the most plausible of all. This recalls the discussion in Chapter 1 concerning the proposal as an *argument* that builds a logical interrelationship among supported assertions, documents conclusions, and presents a summation of how conclusions relate to previous and future research.

Writing the Report. Writing about qualitative data cannot be separated from the analytic process. In fact, it is central to that process, for in the choice of particular words to summarize and reflect the complexity of the data, the researcher is engaging in the interpretive act, lending shape and form— meaning—to massive amounts of raw data.

Several models for report writing exist. Taylor and Bogdan (1984, chaps. 8-12) suggest five different approaches. First is the purely descriptive life history. Here the author presents one person's account of his or her own life, framing that description with analytic points about the social significance of that life. Second is the presentation of data gathered through in-depth interviews and participant observation, where the participants' perspectives are presented, their worldviews forming the structural framework for the report. The third approach attempts to relate practice (the reality of social phenomena) to theory. Here descriptive data are summarized, then linked to more general theoretical constructs. Taylor and Bogdan's fourth approach is the most theoretical. To illustrate it, they provide an example using a study of institutions for individuals with severe cognitive challenges; the report addresses sociological theory about institutionalization and the symbolic management of conditions in total institutions. Their final approach is an attempt to build theory by drawing on data gathered from several types of institutions and under various research conditions. The report they use as an example addresses issues of the presentation of self under various difficult circumstances and attempts to draw theoretical conclusions across types of institutions, types of persons, and types of circumstances.

Van Maanen (1988) identifies three different genres in qualitative writing. *Realist tales* are the most recognized genre, displaying a realist account of the culture under study and published in articles or scholarly monographs in a third-person voice with clear separation between the researcher and the researched. Established by such grandparents of ethnography as Margaret Mead, William Foote Whyte, Howard Becker, and Branislaw Malinowski, this tradition set the standards and criteria for credibility, quality, and respectability in qualitative work. Van Maanen (1988) views these as frequently "flat, dry and sometimes unbearably dull" (p. 48).

Confessional tales are highly personalized accounts with "mini-melodramas of hardships endured in fieldwork" (Van Maanen, 1988, p. 73). This genre aims to display the author's powers of observation and the discipline of good field habits to call attention to the ways building cultural description is part of social science. Powdermaker (1966) is a classical example of this genre.

In *impressionist tales* the field-worker displays her own experiences in the field—a sort of auto-ethnography. Bowen's work (1964) provides a classical example; more current ones include Krieger (1985) and Thorne (1983). The separation of the researcher from the researched is blurred in this genre, and a tale is told through the chronology of fieldwork events, drawing attention to the culture under study but also to the fieldwork experiences that were integral to the cultural description and interpretation.

Into the various phases of data analysis are woven considerations of the soundness and usefulness of the qualitative research study. Some consideration should be given to issues of the value, truthfulness, and soundness of the study throughout the design of the proposal. Considerations of role, for example, should address the personal biography of the researcher and how that might be shaping events and meanings. In what ways is the research, whether participatory or more objectivist, altering the flow of daily life? Similarly, selection of the setting and sampling of people and behaviors within that setting should consider the soundness of those decisions and present a clear rationale that has guided those choices. Chapter 5 continues this discussion of considerations of the soundness and usefulness of the study.

These three chapters have brought the reader through the complex, sometimes tedious process of building a design and choosing research methods for the research study. This section of the proposal should demonstrate that the researcher is competent to conduct the research; knowledgeable about the issues, dilemmas, choices, and decisions to be made in the design and conduct of the research; and immersed in the literature that provides guidance for the qualitative researcher. The research design should be well written and should reveal a sensitivity to various issues, the capacity to be reflective about the nature of inquiry and the substantive questions at hand, and a willingness to tolerate some ambiguity during the conduct of the study. These qualities will stand the researcher in good stead over the course of the research. In addition, however, the researcher should demon-strate some knowledge of the management of resources in the design of a qualitative study. These considerations are discussed in the next chapter.

6 Managing Time and Resources

The process of planning and projecting the resource needs for a qualitative study is an integral aspect of proposal development. The resources most critical to the successful completion of the study are time, personnel, and financial support. Although the last of these is not always readily available, especially in dissertation research, serious consideration must be given to time and personnel. There are also many hidden costs associated with qualitative research that may become apparent only after careful analysis and reflection about the demands of the study.

This chapter provides the researcher with detailed analyses and projections of the resource demands of qualitative research. Using three vignettes as illustrations, we provide general guidelines for consideration in the development and projection of resource needs. Vignette 22 is from Anthony and Rossman's (1991) proposal to evaluate a Commonwealth of Massachusetts's restructuring initiative. This multiperson, multisite, multiyear proposal was developed with ample financial resources and a long time frame for completion of the project. In contrast, Vignette 23 reveals the planning process of a doctoral student proposing a study of recidivism among criminal offenders. This study was a solo venture, with few financial supports to back it up. The contrast between the two is intended to display how each proposal must address difficult resource questions. Finally, Vignette 24 shows how researchers tried to convince a funding agent of the need for financial resources for secondary analyses of qualitative data.

Careful, detailed consideration of the resource demands of a study is critical in demonstrating that the researcher is knowledgeable about qualitative research, understands that the inherent flexibility will create resource difficulties at some point in the study, but has thought through the resource issues and recognizes the demands that will be made.

Some resource decisions cannot be made until basic design issues have been resolved. The researcher, however, should consider resources as she struggles with the conceptual framework and design issues of the study. For example, a researcher cannot decide to conduct a multisite, multiperson project with no prospect of financial resources in sight, nor can she prudently plan to conduct a long-term, intensive participant observation study when she knows she must continue to work full time and cannot possibly devote the necessary time to the study. Thus general resource considerations and design decisions proceed in parallel fashion and are major criteria for the do-ability of the study.

In the narrative structure of the proposal, after discussion of the design of the study, the researcher should address resource needs specifically. These include time demands and management, personnel needs and staffing, and financial support for the entire endeavor. Two vignettes are presented below, followed by a discussion of the major resource needs of each. The vignettes are intended to display the strategies for resource allocation decisions given two quite different studies.

Planning Resources for a Large Study

Although the resource needs for a long-term, complex study are substantially more elaborate than those for dissertation research, the processes of projecting those resources remain very similar. Vignette 22 details how resource decisions were made in planning for a large-scale evaluation of a state restructuring initiative. Titled *Restructuring for the Integration of All Students* (Massachusetts Department of Education [MDOE], 1990a), this discretionary grants program funded seven school districts in the Commonwealth of Massachusetts to encourage experimentation with more fully including students with disabilities as well as those receiving bilingual and compensatory education services in the regular classroom. Each district was awarded grants varying from $25,000 to $125,000 per year for 5 years for this initiative. The Request for Proposals (RFP; Massachusetts Department of Education, 1990b) for an evaluation of this effort stipulated certain design features (qualitative and quantitative methods, for example) and targeted the overall budget at $350,000, although this would be renegotiated each year of the contract.

In designing a proposal to evaluate this restructuring initiative, Anthony and Rossman (1991) had to make careful decisions regarding resource allocations. Several critical resource decisions flowed from the overall design of the study, which had two major components: multisite, multiresearcher, multiyear case studies of implementation in seven school districts; and a cost-benefit analysis of this new, inclusive model of providing categorical services. A study of this scope demanded adequate resources in *time* (sufficient to document implementation at the district and school levels); in *personnel* (capable of thoroughly and efficiently gathering the needed data); and in *financial support* for personnel, travel, data analysis, and report writing.

The first task in projecting resource needs was to organize the study's activities into manageable tasks. These were identified as (1) meetings with Department of Education project staff, (2) meetings of the evaluation team, (3) meetings with district coordinators for feedback, (4) site visits for data gathering, (5) data analysis, and (6) report writing. Initial projections of necessary time were made and then substantially refined, as the associated cost projections were made. That is, initially the research team planned the "ideal study," one in which resources were virtually infinite. At first go-around, this plan called for initial site visits to each district, followed by several site visits during each of the 5 years of the study. Refinements were made when the realistic costs in terms of time, personnel, and travel were estimated. Table 6.1 shows the final allocation of staff days to tasks.

This iterative process characterized all the resource planning activities. As the principal investigators (PIs) identified important aspects of the study that would require time and effort (i.e., more data), the study grew and grew. These ideal projections then had to be grounded in real considerations of the total budget allocated for the study. By making projections based on the study's conceptual framework and the requirements of the RFP, the researchers

Table 6.1 Assignment of Staff and Staff Time to Tasks and Activities

Tasks & Activities		Time Line	Staff and Staff Time (days)		
			PI	Co-PI (days per site)	Evaluators (7)
1. data gathering	Y1	Mar-Jn 91	10	10	12
	Y2	Sep-May 92			16
data analysis		Dec-Jan 92	10		
report preparation		Feb-Mar 92	10	10	
2. preparation for	Y1		4	4	
meetings, meetings,	Y2		10	10	
follow-up memo	Y3		10	10	
preparation	Y4		10	10	
	Y5		10	10	
3. preparation for	Y1		2	2	
meetings, meetings,	Y2		8	8	
follow-up report	Y3		8	8	
preparation	Y4		8	8	
	Y5		8	8	
4. data gathering	Y1	Mar-May 91			6
	Y2	Sep-Apr 92			10
data analysis		Mar-Apr 92		4	5
cost/benefit design		Jly-Jn 92	20		
report preparation		May-Jn 92	10	10	
5. data gathering	Y2	Sep-May 92			10
	Y3	Sep-Apr 93			24
	Y4	Sep-Apr 94			24
data analysis	Y2	Jn-Apr 92	3	5	5
	Y3	Jn-Apr 93	40	30	30
	Y4	Jn-Apr 94	40	30	30
report preparation	Y3	May-Jn 93	10	10	
	Y4	May-Jn 94	10	10	
6. data gathering	Y5	Sep-Dec 94			15
data analysis		Jly-Dec 94	28	28	10
report preparation		Jan-May 95	45	43	
ongoing	Y1		8	8	
administration and	Y2		28	28	
supervision of	Y3		28	28	
grant, including	Y4		28	28	
attendance at bi-	Y5		20	20	
monthly Department					
meetings (Task 2),					
evaluators' group					
meetings (Task 3),					
meetings with					
research assistants					

SOURCE: Anthony & Rossman, Evaluation proposal for *Restructuring for the Integration of All Students*, Massachusetts Department of Education, Malden, 1990, pp. 23-1, 2. Reprinted by permission.

ensured sound adherence to the initial research questions. The following is paraphrased from the evaluation proposal (Anthony & Rossman, 1991) and details the final allocation of resources to each research task.

Vignette 22

Projecting Resources

The evaluation of Restructuring for the Integration of All Students required an approach that would be responsive to the uniqueness of each district and would also provide data useful in formulating policy for all districts. Because it is so difficult to generalize from single cases (Kennedy, 1979), the evaluation focused on cross-site analyses that would identify major patterns (Herriott & Firestone, 1983). This approach recognized the need to inform policy makers about the importance of local variation (Corbett et al., 1984; Rossman et al., 1988) that could not be explored unless the cases were compared. The evaluation, moreover, hoped to provide policy makers with clear descriptions of implementation at the many levels involved in such efforts: district, school, and classroom. The evaluation approach relied on *"nested contexts,"* an approach that gathers data from the multiple levels pertinent to a full understanding of the educational and policy implementation issues of restructuring for integration. Finally, because the phenomenon to be evaluated was complex, multiple evaluation methods were required in order to provide a multifaceted description of restructuring in the seven districts. The use of both qualitative and quantitative data in a *mixed-methods design* (Greene, Caracelli, & Graham, 1989) would enhance the pragmatic usefulness of the evaluation to policy makers (Rossman & Wilson, 1985).

There were two major elements of the evaluation: *case studies* of the seven districts, and the development of a *cost/benefit model and initial analyses* of each district and selected individual students. Each element is detailed below.

Case Studies

The case studies were designed to document the issues and outcomes of implementing comprehensive integration, and focused on the local district as the primary unit of analysis. Because each district's history, culture, capacity and will, resources, and parallel efforts were so different, a district focus would permit full elaboration of those contextual variations that shape policy implementation in important ways. The evaluation team, therefore, planned to concentrate its efforts on each district through four annual site visits to district offices and the sample schools, supplemented by ongoing data collection at the district level. The assumption here was that local variability would profoundly effect the issues addressed and shape local capacity to respond to state policy initiatives (Rossman et al., 1988; Rossman, Corbett, & Dawson, 1986).

District-Level Data Gathering

District-level data gathering would include interviewing central office administrators and gathering district-wide statistical data (for the cost-benefit analyses), and documenting ongoing implementation of the district's initiative over the 5 years of funding. This would entail gathering documents such as teacher minigrant proposals, proposal awards, newsletters, minutes of planning team meetings, documentation of staff development activities, and so on.

This district-level data gathering would provide evidence for the policy formulation and planning processes each district undertook, as well as descriptions of the implementation strategies employed. It would also permit assessments of coordination of services at the district level, as well as organizational strengths and challenges.

School-Level Data Gathering

The school-level analyses were planned to rely on multiple sources of data: in-depth interviews, observations, surveys, and document analysis. At the four annual site visits to each district, the evaluators planned to conduct interviews, observe meetings and classrooms, and gather documents. In-depth interviews would be conducted with building administrators, teachers, students (both regular and those receiving special services), and parents. Attendance at relevant planning meetings would provide additional insight into implementation issues. Observations of classrooms would be made, focusing on the developing opportunities for regular education children and children with disabilities to interact. These qualitative data would be supplemented with surveys of all teachers in the sample schools and a randomly selected sample of parents from each school to provide breadth of understanding of various role groups' perspectives. Finally, school-level documents (financial, minutes of meetings, memoranda, program description, for example) would be gathered to elaborate further an understanding of local implementation. An assessment of the technical assistance needed from the Department of Education (DOE) would also be made, as required by the RFP, based on the resource analysis and survey results described above.

School Selection Strategy. Selection of schools within districts was planned to follow each district's implementation plan, focusing on the levels selected by each. Sampling of schools, of classrooms, and of individual teachers, counselors, and students within schools for interviewing and observation would be purposive (Patton, 1980). Generally, the proposal design was to include one high school, one middle/junior high school, and two or three elementary schools. This selection strategy recognized the benefits accruing to studying a small number of schools in depth; the associated loss is of broader data across a number of schools. An in-depth assessment of three or four schools per district was reasoned to be most consistent with the philosophy of the restructuring initiative.

Refinement of Research Design

Regular refinement of the research design was built into the proposed research schedule. The primary purpose of this activity was to create structured opportunities to communicate with important audiences for feedback about the research, notable the DOE and the districts involved. The underlying premise for formally building into the schedule opportunities for refinement was simply that a project of this scope required the regular rethinking and adjustment of efforts consistent with a formative evaluation.

Data Management

The fieldwork would generate a considerable amount of data that would demand a management system. First, original field notes would be stored by site and by round of fieldwork. Second, after each trip, field notes would be reorganized around a set of categories deriving from the research questions. Of course, these categories would be revised to reflect additional data that did not fit initial questions. This process would serve as a crude but effective coding system. These documents would be typed to facilitate use by all members of the research team. Third, two sets of memoranda files would be kept. One would be for substantive issues. In this file, researchers would maintain a running dialogue of issues to consider and interesting events to note. The second would be for methodological issues. These memoranda would focus on the progress and problems of the fieldwork, providing important information relevant to the research reports.

Data Analysis

Data analysis would rely on three mechanisms to ensure rich and authentic descriptions of the schools and districts as inclusion initiatives were being implemented. The first would be regularly scheduled meetings of the research team. The purposes of these meetings would be (1) to keep the team members aware of the fieldwork at all the sites; (2) to discuss emerging issues, concerns, hypotheses, or data collection problems; and (3) to ensure, through feedback among the team, that comparable data collection activities went on at all the sites.

The second mechanism would be analytic memoranda. These memoranda would be drafted by team members and would serve as guides for further exploration of categories in the field, as checks on the site-specific data collected, and as verification of emerging hypotheses. They would also serve as the basis for discussion at the team meetings.

Finally, the evaluation would result in several case studies and cross-site reports. The case studies would offer rich detail about specific school and district implementation activities. They would be shared with participants in the study to sharpen the analysis by incorporating participants' views as validity checks and to engage participants in the study. The primary analytic focus, however, would be on cross-site reports. These would be organized around the important dimensions described in the conceptual portion of the proposal as shaping substantial change: the political, technical, and cultural.

The processes of data analysis would entail three activities: data reduction, data display, and conclusion drawing/verification. These activities would proceed concurrently during the research project, although any one might take precedence over the others at various times.

Data reduction would begin as soon as the important topics or themes were identified and continue throughout data collection and report writing. Each choice or research decision (whether of topic, site, person to interview, or what to record as field notes) would involve data reduction because it would be a narrowing, a selecting from all possible choices (Miles & Huberman, 1993). Other instances of data reduction would occur during the coding of data and report writing. Each reduction act would help to bring the masses of data into more manageable proportion, thereby making them easier to comprehend and work with. It would be important, however, to remain open to the novel or unexpected insight that might emerge.

The plan described data display as the process of presenting the data. For qualitative data, display would usually take the narrative form. Qualitative data also might be displayed in graphic formats such as matrices, charts, graphs, and tables, however. Displaying data in these structures would force the researchers to consider what was known and not known about the phenomenon in question, and could suggest new relationships, propositions, and explanations for further analysis. Thus data display could promote analysis by disciplining the researcher to identify what was known and not known about the setting and could also summarize the results of analysis. The study would include classical narrative displays of ideal types, but might also entail the use of charts and graphs as suggested by Miles and Huberman (1984), although the exact form would depend on the data.

Drawing conclusions and verifying them was also seen to take place before, during, and after data collection. Before data collection the researchers would have vague and unformed hunches that could lead to conclusions. As analysis proceeded, however, these conclusions would be tested out and elaborated systematically for their soundness and sturdiness. The conclusions would become more explicit as they were verified by the data in increasingly grounded analyses.

The proposal described data reduction, data display, and conclusion drawing/verification as the activities of data analysis occurring iteratively throughout the study. Rather than suggesting that each type of activity might occur at a specific phase of the research process, the proposal highlighted how the activities would interrelate and feed one another. Data display might spur conclusions that then require verification; data reduction through coding might suggest a particular format that would make the data more comprehensible. Thus each set of activities would feed the others interactively; all three would combine to present a comprehensive and robust explanation of the successes and challenges of implementing inclusion initiatives.

Reports

The RFP required regular reporting to the Department of Education: regular meetings followed by memoranda of understanding; a baseline report; annual reports; and a final, summative report. The annual reports were envisioned as comprehensive, book-length documents summarizing initiatives in each district, profiling certain statistical information and providing cross-case analyses in the form of an executive summary. In addition, the evaluators planned to ensure that, with award of the contract, independent publication could be pursued in both academic and practitioner-oriented journals. In addition, dissemination was planned to include presentations at professional meetings (e.g., the meetings of the American Educational Research Association) and to staff at the sites under study. The final product was proposed as a book-length document describing the entire project.

The entire scope of evaluation activities, "deliverables" (written memoranda and reports), and their attendant costs were projected through three tables. The first projected the assignment of staff and staff time to specific tasks and activities, and is reproduced as Table 6.1. This table presented the person-days necessary for the completion of the various activities of the evaluation. The second table reorganized this information and presented it as by year, thereby projecting the personnel and time necessary for each year's activities; it is reproduced as Table 6.2. Finally, the proposal included a time line that projected the flow of activities over the course of the evaluation, and is presented as Figure 6.1.

Time

As Vignette 22 illustrates, projecting sufficient time to undertake a full and richly detailed study that also remains doable is a difficult task but one that can be rewarding. Thinking through the time necessary for various research activities

Table 6.2   Staff and Staff Time by Year and Task

	PI	Co-PI	Evaluators (7)
		(days per site)	
Year 1, March-June 1991			
Task 1	10	10	12
Task 2	4	4	
Task 3	2	2	
Task 4			6
oversight and administration	2	2	
Totals	18	18	18
Year 2, July-June 1992			
Task 1	20	10	16
Task 2	10	10	
Task 3	8	8	
Task 4	30	14	15
Task 5	3	5	15
oversight and administration	10	10	
Totals	81	57	46
Year 3, July-June 1993			
Task 2	10	10	
Task 3	8	8	
Task 5	50	30	54
oversight and administration	10	10	
Totals	78	58	54
Year 4, July-June 1994			
Task 2	10	10	
Task 3	8	8	
Task 5	50	30	54
oversight and administration	10	10	
Totals	78	58	54
Year 5, July-June 1995			
Task 2	10	10	
Task 3	8	8	
Task 6	55	42	25
oversight and administration	10	10	
Totals	83	70	25

SOURCE: Anthony & Rossman, Evaluation Proposal for *Restructuring for the Integration of All Students,* Massachusetts Department of Education, Malden, 1990, pp. 23-3, 4. Reprinted by permission.

can be sobering to experienced researchers, whereas the novice becomes more realistic through this discipline. For example, each of the research tasks described in this vignette required a certain number of days for its successful completion. The first step in projecting time demands was to determine the optimal number of days for each site visit. Although this depended on the year of the study, the

Month	July	Aug	Sep	Oct	Nov	Dec	Jan	Feb	Mar	Apr	May	June
Task												
Year 1												
DoE meetings									x		x	
evaluators' meetings											x	
RAs' meetings								x		x		
data gathering										─	─	─
data analysis												
Year 2												
DoE meetings		x		x		x		x		x		x
evaluators' meetings					x						x	
RAs' meetings			x		x		x		x		x	
data gathering			─	─	─	─	─	─	─			
data analysis		─	─	─	─	─	─	─	─	─	─	
report preparation	─	─							D─	─	─	─D
Years 3 & 4												
DoE meetings		x		x		x		x		x		x
evaluators' meetings		x			x			x			x	
RAs' meetings			x		x		x		x		x	
data gathering			─	─	─	─	─	─	─			
data analysis		─	─	─	─	─	─	─	─	─	─	
report preparation	─	─									─	─D
Year 5												
DoE meetings	x	x		x		x		x		x	x	x
evaluators' meetings		x			x			x			x	
RAs' meetings			x		x	x						
data gathering			─	─	─	─						
data analysis	─	─	─	─	─	─						
report preparation									─	─	─	─D

Figure 6.1. Time Line for Completion of Tasks and Deliverables

SOURCE: Anthony & Rossman, Evaluation proposal for *Restructuring for the Integration of All Students*, Massachusetts Department of Education, Malden, 1990, pp. 23-25. Reprinted by permission.

evaluation team was able to estimate days by deciding on the number of interviews possible in each school, the hours to allocate for observations, the amount of time necessary to talk with the central office staff, and the amount of time needed to gather documents and other archival data.

In qualitative proposals, the number of days allocated to data gathering becomes a metric for estimating the time required for other tasks, such as data management, analysis, and report writing. That is, the amount of data gathered dictates the amount of time needed to manage and analyze those data. Once the researcher has projected time for fieldwork, a management

. The projections developed for Table 6.1 helped
.ork for estimating costs, discussed below.
.er should also use this kind of framework to address practical
. time management chart, research agenda, calendar of research
.escription of research phases, or some other concrete plan shows a
.g agent or dissertation committee that the researcher has thought
.ugh the specific people, settings, events, and data involved in conducting
. research. This demonstrates that the research is feasible. But the researcher
.hould remind the reader that this plan is a guide; it is a tentative road map
that will most likely undergo some modifications as data are collected and
analyzed and as new patterns for more focused data collection become apparent. The chart serves as a guide for initial contacts and reminds the reader of
the inherently flexible nature of qualitative research.

Personnel

The allocations of time to tasks also shapes decisions about personnel
needs. In Vignette 22, as the scope of the study developed (number of sites,
single- or multiple-person research teams), personnel decisions could be
made. The principal investigators, by university contract, could allocate the
equivalent of the summer months and one day per week to the effort. Their
time would be supplemented by a cadre of graduate students who would
be awarded research assistantships to work on the project for no more than
20 hours per week for the academic year, with additional summer funding
budgeted into the proposal. These person-loadings are seen in the budget
for the evaluation, presented as Table 6.3.

Financial Resources

For dissertation research or sole-investigator studies, analyzing tasks can
help the researcher decide to purchase certain services; for example, audio-
tape transcription or data processing. This analysis can also introduce the
novice to the variety of tasks associated with the project. Determination of
the resources necessary for the conduct of the study must often wait until
fundamental design decisions have been made. Those design choices,
however, must be made with some knowledge about the finances available
to support the study. In the vignette above, the evaluators knew that they
were constrained by a total budget (direct costs) of approximately $100,000

Table 6.3 Budget Summary (in dollars)

Item	Yr 1	Yr 2	Yr 3	Yr 4	Yr 5
Personnel	15,442.0	56,424.0	56,116.0	55,726.0	47,140.0
Travel	1,819.4	4,516.6	4,675.0	4,675.0	2,200.0
Telephone & Consumable Sup.	540.0	1,975.0	1,964.0	1,950.0	1,650.0
Photocopying	463.0	2,821.0	1,683.0	1,672.0	2,357.0
Postage	49.5	1,650.0	49.5	49.5	49.5
Equipment	5,000.0				
Totals	21,683.9	67,386.6	64,487.5	64,072.5	53,396.5
Total Request:	271,027				

SOURCE: Anthony & Rossman, Evaluation proposal for *Restructuring for the Integration of All Students,* Massachusetts Department of Education, Malden, 1990, p. 27-1. Adapted by permission.

per year, but that this would extend over 5 years. Because the contract was renegotiated each year, moreover, there was the possibility of increasing that amount (or of having it reduced!).

Though this may seem a considerable sum to the novice proposal writer, planning a multisite, multiyear study with intensive data gathering as a primary design goal became quite difficult within this budget. Travel and personnel costs would increase with inflation and rising salaries (hopefully!). Direct personnel and travel costs represented a substantial proportion of the total budget.

The other major costs associated with the evaluation activities included (1) equipment (computers, fax machine); (2) office supplies, telephones, and postage; (3) books and subscriptions; (4) printing and duplicating; and (5) contracted services (tape transcription, computerized data analysis, consultants). As the costs of computer time vary considerably, the proposal writer should consult local costs and time allocations in developing that portion of a qualitative proposal. The time required for thorough transcription also varies: Each hour of tape requires from 3 or 4 hours to 7 or 8 hours for transcription. Thus the cost of tape transcription could vary enormously; at either end, however, it is very expensive.

Planning Dissertation Research

Many of the same issues confronted in the large-scale evaluation project are apparent in Vignette 23, which was a proposal for dissertation research.

Although the scope was considerably smaller, similar resource challenges emerged in planning the study.

Vignette 23

Feasibility and Planning for Qualitative Research

"Should I do a study that is clean, relatively quick, limited, and do-able so as to finish and get on with my professional life, or should I do something I really want to do that may be messy and unclear but would be challenging and new enough to sustain my interest?" (Hammonds-White, personal communication, August 5, 1987)

A doctoral student, finding any number of stumbling blocks standing between her and the completion of her dissertation project, was asked to reflect on the process through which the research plan had been developed. Her response indicated that, as with one who prepares to make any kind of major investment, a preliminary notion of how to proceed should be tempered by a comparison of anticipated costs and available resources. In this student's case, she had to weigh energy (the researcher's physical and emotional stamina), time, and finances.

The demands of the student's chosen research methods were many. Seeking to explore a process, she chose naturalistic inquiry—which would encourage her to search for multiple views of reality and the ways such views were constructed. Her training, experience, and interest in counseling psychology, coupled with a positive assessment of her knowledge and competence in this field, constituted excellent sources of personal energy. This was an area of particular interest (the want-to-do-ability); methods were elegantly suited to that substantive focus. The researcher realized, however, that personal energy and a deep commitment to the topic were not going to be sufficient.

She looked to the university for two types of support that she described as "risk-taking" support and "learning" support. The first type of support would offer encouragement to someone attempting to go beyond the conventional in his or her research. The second type was offered by faculty members who possessed the interests and the skills necessary to advise her.

In addition to personal energy and commitment and faculty support, a third source of energy was a support group made up of others who were engaged in dissertation research. Of that group she wrote: "We meet every other week, set short-term goals for ourselves, and help each other with the emotional highs and lows of the process."

The commitment of time required of an individual doing qualitative research is substantial. This particular researcher was quick to advise that those following similar research plans would do well to build into their proposals more time than they thought would be required, in order to make allowances for the unexpected. In her case, a change in her family situation necessitated a return to full-time employment, thus suspending her research when it was only two-thirds complete.

In addition, financial resources need to be equal to the financial demands of a study. When it appeared unlikely that grant monies would be available to finance her research, the student opted for a smaller-scale study that she could finance personally.

Vignette 23 should stress the importance of being practical and realistic. Although it is impossible to anticipate all of the potential stumbling blocks, a thoughtful and thorough research proposal will address the issue of feasibility by making an honest assessment of available energy, time, and financial resources and requirements.

During the planning for and conduct of the above study, several resource issues became apparent. First, the commitment to a research project that is a graduate student's dissertation research is different from the commitment required of the researchers in Vignette 22. A dissertation carries both professional and personal significance that few subsequent research projects will. Furthermore, the project described in Vignette 22 had built-in supports for the researchers. As a team project funded by an external agent, commitments to colleagues as well as professional responsibilities to the funding agent were adequate to sustain commitment and rebuild interest when it began to wane. A dissertation demands different kinds of supports; the most important are those of mentors and peers.

Mentors and Peers

In planning qualitative dissertation research, support from university faculty to make judgments about the adequacy of the proposal is crucial. At least one committee member, preferably the chair, should have had experience conducting qualitative studies. Such experience should also help in making decisions about how to allocate time realistically to various tasks, given that all-important idea that qualitative research often takes much more time than one might predict. Faculty support and encouragement are critical for developing research proposals that are substantial, elegant, and doable, and for advocacy in the larger university community to legitimize this particular study and qualitative research generally.

The experiences of our graduate students suggest that the support of peers is crucial for the personal and emotional sustenance that students find so valuable in negotiating among faculty whose requests and demands may be in conflict with one another. Graduate seminars or advanced courses in qualitative methods provide excellent structures for formal discussions as students deal with issues arising from role management to grounded theory-building in their dissertations. Student support groups also build in a commitment to others not unlike that found in the team project described in Vignette 22. By establishing deadlines and commitments to one another, students become more efficient and productive. These groups bridge the "existential aloneness" of the conduct of dissertation research.

Time on a Small Scale

Developing a qualitative dissertation proposal demands sensitivity to the time necessary for the thorough completion of the project. This is where the experience of mentors on the university faculty becomes crucial. Gaining access to a setting can take 6 months or more and may require the skills of a diplomat. As in Vignette 23, personal circumstances may intervene to alter dramatically the student's available time and energy to conduct the study. Thus, even though not all critical events can be anticipated, planning for more time than initially appears necessary is prudent.

Financing

In some fields (notably, mental health, anthropology, and international education), financial support may be available through federal agencies or private foundations for dissertation research. Unfortunately, this is not typically the case in most social science fields, in education, or in other applied fields. Opportunities sometimes become available, however, to work on a university professor's funded grant as a research assistant. Such was the case in Vignette 22, which supported four graduate students annually, several of whom dovetailed their research interests with those of the project.

Much more common, especially in education, is the case in Vignette 23, where the student had to modify the proposed research to conform to the personal financial resources she was able to devote to the project. Recall that this same process occurred in the funded research described in Vignette 22. The researchers planned the ideal study based on design considerations and the purposes of the study, and then had to modify that ideal design based on the real budgetary constraints under which they operated.

In the conduct of dissertation research there are many costs, some obvious and some hidden, that will arise over the course of the study. Planning ahead for these makes them less of a surprise and therefore a bit more manageable. These costs cluster into three categories: materials, services, and personal.

Materials. The materials necessary for the completion of a dissertation include word-processing equipment and materials, note cards and filing systems, tape recorders and tapes, video equipment and cameras, books, articles, and copies of completed dissertations. The student should project the costs in each category, being sure to include photocopying costs for journal articles, drafts of the work as it proceeds, and copies of the final document.

Services. The services necessary for the completion of the dissertation vary depending upon the skills of the student. Typical services, however, might include tape transcribing, word processing, statistical data analysis consulting, and professional proofreading and editing. At the end of the work, the student often wants to have copies of the work professionally bound; this is an additional service that might be important for the student to consider in projecting overall costs.

Personal Costs. Personal costs are the most difficult to specify but may also be the most important in terms of perceived costs to the individual student. Dissertation work is unlike any the student has ever undertaken: It is not like a large course; it is not like reading for exams—it is of quite a different magnitude than either of those. The sustained effort necessary to complete the project takes time away from all the other commitments in the student's life, whether these are work, family, friends, or professional associations and volunteer groups. Students who are the most successful in moving through the phases are those who build support networks for themselves within their families or through friends and colleagues. Even though not all the costs associated with personal sacrifice can be anticipated, knowledge that the undertaking is not trivial and will require sacrifices on the part of the student can make the entire process more manageable.

Sometimes researchers seek new funds to continue a project that uncovered interesting data. It is difficult to convince funding agency reviewers that a reworking of data analysis is a worthwhile venture. Vignette 24 describes a researcher trying to convince funding agency reviewers that secondary analysis of qualitative data required resources.

Vignette 24

Walking the Reviewers Through Qualitative Analysis

The data collected were voluminous—comparative qualitative and quantitative data from key state education policy makers in six states. From a study funded by the National Institute of Education, Mitchell, Wirt, and Marshall (1986) developed a taxonomy of state mechanisms for influencing school programs and practices, and showed the effect of political culture and the relative power of education policy makers to affect the choices made in state capitals. Captivated by the richness of the interview data, Marshall began to develop a grounded theory of assumptive worlds—understandings that policy makers have about the way things are done, as demonstrated in their stories. Although this theory had been published (Marshall, Mitchell, & Wirt, 1985, 1986), Marshall knew it needed further development and refinement. She sought funding from the National Science Foundation's Political Science Program, promising a secondary analysis of the interview data from six states that would rely on the software program *Ethnograph* (Qualis Research Associates, 1987) as a tool, and would elaborate the theory derived from early analysis. The funding could be low, because no new data collection was required.

Months later, the reviewers came back. One reviewer said, "This proposal breaks fresh and important ground in the political field." Another noted that, "Using qualitative data in a systematic way and employing computers in data management are innovative techniques well worth development." A third said, however, "The proposal is to apply qualitative analysis to the interview materials. Perhaps that term has some [other] understood connotation in other research traditions, but so far as I could fathom what it means is the investigator would read/listen to interview materials and file them on a micro computer." The proposal was rejected.

Overcoming frustration, Marshall decided to revise and resubmit her proposal. In the new proposal, she made these important changes. First, in the theoretical framework, related literature, and significance, she created a chart, tracing the precise place where assumptive worlds fit with other political science and education policy theory and literature. Second, while retaining the section explaining the traditions of qualitative research, she connected this directly to quotes where *political scientists* had called for more theory building with comparable case studies and where they had bemoaned the fact that political scientists are good at identifying structures, but they need to get behind the scenes and into the ways in which the values of the policy culture affect policy outcomes. Third, she retained the table (see Table 6.4) that demonstrated the promise, derived from the preliminary analysis, of the theory. In text she described its significance for understanding the policy culture. Finally, and perhaps most important, following a section on the philosophy of qualitative methodology and a section on the use of microcomputers with qualitative data, she wrote the following step-by-step description:

> Qualitative data analysis and the development of grounded theory (Glaser & Strauss, 1967) seem to be mystical processes to those accustomed to statistical analysis. However, the goal of both method-ologies are the same—to identify clear and consistent patterns of phenomena by a systematic process. I will follow the following steps:
>
> 1. Transcribe data in *Ethnograph* files, using categories from preliminary analysis and from literature review, noted earlier.
> 2. Develop hypotheses on assumptive world effects on policy outcomes from field notes and interview data, based on analytic notes regarding "assumptive worlds" (already started with West Virginia and Pennsylvania data).
> 3. Test these hypotheses about assumptive worlds by examining all computer files with relevant descriptors. For example, when identifying patterns of behavior in legislative-state board relations, call up all files under the

Table 6.4   Functions of the Operative Principles of Assumptive Worlds

Action Guide Domains and Operational Principles	Maintain Power and Predictability	Promote Cohesion
Who has the right and responsibility to initiate?		
the prescription for the CSSO role	x	
the prescription for the SDE role	x	
legislative—SDE role	x	
variations in initiative in legislature	x	
What policy ideas are deemed unacceptable?		
policies that trample on powerful interests		x
policies that lead to open defiance		x
policies that defy tradition and dominant interests		x
policy debates that diverge from the prevailing value		x
untested, "unworkable" policy		x
What uses of power in policy-making activities are appropriate?		
know your place and cooperate with the powerful	x	
something for everyone	x	
touch all the bases	x	
bet on the winner	x	
limits on social relationships	x	
constraints on staffers	x	
work with constraints and tricks		x
policy actors' sponsorship of policy issue network		x
uses of interstate comparison		x
What are the special state conditions affecting policy?		
cultural characteristics		x
geographic, demographic characteristics		x

SOURCE: C. Marshall, grant proposal to National Science Foundation, 1988.

descriptor, state board, or, when identifying constraints on legislative staffers, call up all field notes and quotations under that label.

4. Obtain field notes and taped interviews from Wisconsin, Illinois, Arizona, and California.

5. Content analyze all six states' data in order to (a) identify any additional patterns of behavior or belief not evident from the initial analysis, and (b) identify redefinitions of domains and operational principles.

6. Re-analyze the file data using the alterations of assumptive world domains and operational principles.

7. Continue to reorder the six states' files until clear, mutually exclusive and exhaustive categories of behavior and belief systems are identified that organize the data descriptions of the policy environment.

Such description was required, she now understood.

Vignette 24 outlined that experienced qualitative researchers understand the labor intensiveness of qualitative data analysis and that it requires time and money. Those more attuned to traditional research, however, may need explicit details before they will provide support for that labor. Funding agencies, pressed by the needs of many eager researchers and guided by the peer review process, will not provide resources unless everyone involved can see *clearly* how the money will be converted into knowledge. Even small requests for a graduate assistant or a computer program will be denied if the research sounds like a mystical process or if it sounds like simple filing. Anyone who has ever done qualitative data analysis knows better, but those with the funds need explicit guidance so they can see how the expenditure is justified. Vignette 24 demonstrates the need to fit explanations to the knowledge bases and predilections of reviewers, thereby providing assurances that the researcher *can* produce something meaningful on their terms and walking them through the steps to be followed.

This chapter has displayed the iterative processes of planning sufficient resources to support the conduct of a qualitative research project. Vignette 22 could aptly be retitled "Planning in a Context of Largess," because the study was conceived in the midst of adequate financial resources. The major problem for that study was paring down the ideal design to conform to those budget parameters.

Vignette 23 portrayed some of the unique problems associated with planning dissertation research, in which financial resources are largely unavailable and where time and personal support systems become critical. Each type of project has unique challenges when the researcher is designing the proposal. Consideration of these issues strengthens the proposal by demonstrating that the researcher is aware of and sensitive to the many challenges that may arise during the conduct of the study. Finally, Vignette 24 reminds us that even low-budget studies will be criticized if they cannot lead the reviewers to an understanding of the resources needed for qualitative analysis. Attention to these considerations helps strengthen the overall proposal and makes its positive evaluation more likely.

Throughout this book, we have presented considerations for building clear, thorough, and thoughtful proposals for qualitative research. In the final chapter, we make these considerations more explicit by describing them as a set of criteria.

7
Defending the Value and Logic of Qualitative Research

Writers of qualitative research proposals should be concerned with developing a sound rationale for the choice of methods in the proposal. Although this must be demonstrated for any research proposal, with qualitative proposals the need may be especially acute. Unfortunately, qualitative research does not yet have the general acceptance that quantitative paradigms enjoy and, therefore, more attention should be devoted to a sound rationale than with more traditional proposals.

Developing a logic that will solidly defend the proposal entails two large domains: responding to criteria for the soundness of the project; and demonstrating the usefulness of the proposed work to the conceptual framework and research questions posed initially. Careful consideration of each of these domains will help the proposal writer develop a logic for the defense of the proposal.

Criteria of Soundness

All research must respond to canons that stand as criteria against which the trustworthiness of the project can be evaluated. These canons can be phrased as questions to which all research must respond (Lincoln & Guba, 1985). First, how credible are the particular findings of the study? By what criteria can we judge them? Second, how transferable and applicable are these findings to another setting or group of people? Third, how can we be reasonably sure that the findings would be replicated if the study were conducted with the same participants in the same context? And, fourth, how can we be sure that the findings are reflective of the subjects and the inquiry itself rather than a creation of the researcher's biases or prejudices?

Lincoln and Guba (1985) refer to these questions as establishing the "truth value" (p. 290) of the study, its applicability, consistency, and neutrality. Every systematic inquiry into the human condition must address these issues. Although Lincoln and Guba match these terms to the conventional positivist paradigm—internal validity, external validity, reliability, and objectivity—they then demonstrate how inappropriate these constructs are for naturalistic or qualitative inquiry.

Lincoln and Guba propose four alternative constructs that more accurately reflect the assumptions of the qualitative paradigm. The first is *credibility,* in which the goal is to demonstrate that the inquiry was conducted in such a manner as to ensure that the subject was accurately identified and described. The inquiry then must be "credible to the constructors of the original multiple realities" (1985, p. 296).

The strength of the qualitative study that aims to explore a problem or describe a setting, a process, a social group, or a pattern of interaction will be its validity. An in-depth description showing the complexities of variables and interactions will be so embedded with data derived from the setting that it cannot help but be valid. Within the parameters of that setting, population, and theoretical framework, the research will be valid. A qualitative researcher should therefore adequately state those parameters, thereby placing boundaries around the study.

The second construct Lincoln and Guba propose is *transferability,* in which the burden of demonstrating the applicability of one set of findings to another context rests more with the investigator who would make that transfer than with the original investigator. Kennedy (1979) refers to this as the second decision span in generalizing. That is, the first decision span allows the researcher to generalize the findings about a particular sample to the population from which that sample was drawn (assuming adequate population specification and random selection of the sample). The second decision span occurs when an investigator wants to apply the findings about the population of interest to a second population believed or presumed sufficiently similar to the first to warrant that application. This second decision span entails judgments about the relevancy of the first study to the second setting.

A qualitative study's transferability or generalizability to other settings may be problematic. The generalization of qualitative findings to other populations, settings, and treatment arrangements—that is, its *external validity*—is seen by traditional canons as a weakness in the approach. To counter challenges, the researcher can refer back to the original theoretical framework to show how data collection and analysis will be guided by concepts and models. By doing so, the researcher states the theoretical parameters of the research. Then those who make policy or design research studies within those same parameters can determine whether or not the cases described can be generalized for new research policy and transferred to other settings, while the reader or user of specific research can see how research ties into a body of theory.

For example, a case study of implementation of a new staff development program in a high school can be tied into theory of implementation of innovations in organizations, leadership, personnel management, and adult career socialization theory. Then the research can be used in planning program policy and further research in a variety of settings, not just limited to the high school, not limited to school organizations, and not limited to staff development. It can be included with research about organizations; it can build a bridge to organizational theory.

One additional strategic choice can enhance a study's generalizability: triangulating multiple sources of data. Triangulation is the act of bringing more than one source of data to bear on a single point. Derived from navigation science, the concept has been fruitfully applied to social science inquiry (see Denzin, 1978; Jick, 1979; Rossman & Wilson, 1985, 1994). Data from different sources can be used to corroborate, elaborate, or illuminate the research in question (Rossman & Wilson, 1985). Designing a study in which multiple cases, multiple informants, or more than one data gathering method are used can greatly strengthen the study's usefulness for other settings.

The third construct is *dependability,* in which the researcher attempts to account for changing conditions in the phenomenon chosen for study as well as changes in the design created by increasingly refined understanding of the setting. This represents a set of assumptions very different from those shaping the concept of reliability. Positivist notions of reliability assume an unchanging universe where inquiry could, quite logically, be replicated. This assumption of an unchanging social world is in direct contrast to the qualitative/interpretive assumption that the social world is always being constructed, and the concept of replication is itself problematic.

The final construct, *confirmability,* captures the traditional concept of objectivity. Lincoln and Guba stress the need to ask whether the findings of the study could be confirmed by another. By doing so, they remove evaluation from some inherent characteristic of the researcher (objectivity) and place it squarely on the data themselves. Thus the qualitative criterion is: Do the data help confirm the general findings and lead to the implications? This is the appropriate qualitative criterion.

A qualitative research proposal should respond to concerns that the natural subjectivity of the researcher will shape the research. Again, the researcher should assert the strengths of the qualitative study. She should gain some understanding, even empathy, for the research participants in order to gain entry into their world. The researcher's insights increase the likelihood that she will be able to describe the complex social system being studied. The researcher, however, should build in strategies for balancing bias in interpretation. Such controls would include the following:

- A research partner or a person who plays "devil's advocate" and critically questions the researcher's analyses
- A constant search for negative instances (see Glaser & Strauss, 1967)
- Checking and rechecking the data and purposeful examination of possible rival hypotheses
- Practicing value-free note-taking, then taking two sets of notes, one with more objective observation and another that allows the researcher to impose some conceptual scheme or metaphor, and to be creative with the data in ways that might prove useful for more formal analysis (Schatzman & Strauss, 1973, outline a useful note-taking technique that facilitates analysis)
- Devising tests to check analyses and applying the tests to the data, asking questions of the data
- Following the guidance of previous researchers to control for data quality (McCall & Simmons, 1969, have collected the advice of previous researchers)

- Conducting an audit of the data collection and analytic strategies (see Lincoln & Guba, 1985)

The qualitative researcher should be familiar with the issues in data quality control and analysis and should display an ability to develop strategies that are appropriate to the research.

Clearly, criteria of goodness for qualitative research differ from the criteria developed for experimental and positivist research. Still, it is helpful to articulate the parallels and differences. Qualitative research does not pretend to be replicable. The researcher purposefully avoids controlling the research conditions and concentrates on recording the complexity of situational contexts and interrelations as they occur. The researcher's goal of discovering this complexity by altering research strategies within a flexible research design, moreover, cannot be replicated by future researchers, nor should it be attempted.

Qualitative researchers can respond to the traditional social science concern for replicability, however, by taking the following steps. First, they can assert that qualitative studies by their nature (and, really, all research) cannot be replicated because the real world changes. Second, by keeping thorough notes and a journal or log that records each design decision and the rationale behind it, researchers allow others to inspect their procedures, protocols, and decisions. Finally, by keeping all collected data in well-organized, retrievable form, researchers can make them available easily if the findings are challenged or if another researcher wants to reanalyze the data.

Marshall (1985a) recommends additional criteria for assessing the value and trustworthiness of qualitative research. Although these criteria were developed to apply to written reports of qualitative research, they are relevant for proposal developers as well. Attention to these standards helps ensure a sound and reasonable research proposal. Marshall (1990) lists 20 standards for judging qualitative study reports, arguing that proposal writers should design, conduct, and report their studies with these criteria in mind:

I suggest that we would agree on common criteria (although different paradigms would weight each criterion differently). Most of us in judging the goodness of qualitative studies would look for the following evidence:

(1) The method is explicated in detail so the reader can judge whether it was adequate and makes sense. An articulate rationale for the use of

qualitative methods is given so that skeptics will accept the approach. The methods for attaining entry and managing role, data collection, recording, analysis, ethics, and exit are discussed. There is an audability trail—a running record of procedures (often done in an appendix)— and there is description of how the site and sample were selected. Data collection and analysis procedures are public, not magical.

(2) Assumptions are stated. Biases are expressed, and the researcher does a kind of self-analysis for personal biases and a framework analysis for theoretical biases.

(3) The research guards against value judgments in data collection and in analysis (i.e., avoiding transgressions like Whyte's, 1955, judgmental field notes about "dilapidated houses" in *Street Corner Society*).

(4) There is abundant evidence from raw data to demonstrate the connection between the presented findings and the real world, and the data are presented in readable, accessible form, perhaps aided by graphics, models, charts, and figures.

(5) The research questions are stated, and the study answers those questions and generates further questions.

(6) The relationship between this study and previous studies is explicit. Definitions of phenomena are provided, with explicit reference to previously identified phenomena, but it is clear that the research goes beyond previously established frameworks—challenging old ways of thinking.

(7) The study is reported in a manner that is accessible to other researchers, practitioners, and policymakers. It makes adequate translation of findings so that others will be able to use the findings in a timely way.

(8) Evidence is presented showing that the researcher was tolerant of ambiguity, searched for alternative explanations, checked out negative instances, and used a variety of methods to check the findings (i.e., triangulation).

(9) The report acknowledges the limitations of generalizability while assisting the readers in seeing the transferability of findings.

(10) It is clear that there was a phase of "first days in the field" in which a problem focus was generated from observation, not from library research. In other words, it is a study that is an exploration, not merely a study to find contextual data to verify old theories.

(11) Observations are made (or sampled) of a full range of activities over a full cycle of activities.

(12) Data are preserved and available for reanalysis.

(13) methods are devised for checking data quality (e.g., informants' knowledgeability, ulterior motives, and truthfulness) and for guarding against ethnocentric explanations.

(14) In-field work analysis is documented.

(15) Meaning is elicited from cross-cultural perspectives.

(16) The researcher is careful about sensitivity of those being researched—ethical standards are maintained.

(17) People in the research setting benefit in some way (ranging from getting a free meal or an hour of sympathetic listening to being empowered to throw off their chains).

(18) Data collection strategies are the most adequate and efficient available. There is evidence that the researcher is a finely tuned research instrument, whose personal talents, experiential biases, and insights are used consciously. The researcher is careful to be self-analytical and recognize when she or he is getting subjective or going native.

(19) The study is tied into "the big picture." The researcher looks holistically at the setting to understand linkages among systems.

(20) The researcher traces the historical context to understand how institutions and roles have evolved. (pp. 193-195)

Attention to all 20 criteria ensures a solid qualitative proposal that displays concern for issues of trustworthiness and shows how knowledgeable the proposal writer is regarding these several issues. We recommend that the proposal writer incorporate sections dealing with these issues. Some will already have been addressed in the body of the proposal; others should be discussed explicitly either in the proposal or in the defense of the proposal. (See Marshall, 1985b, 1990, for a discussion of the evolving set of "criteria of goodness" that cut across scholarly and political debates.)

Finally, researchers need to allay the fears (both their own and those of their reviewers) that they might become stalled when faced with analyzing the data. Again, a pilot study, a hypothesized model, or an outline of possible data analysis categories (as illustrated in Table 3.1, in Chapter 3) can be appended to the proposal. The qualitative researcher should always caution that such models, outlines, and categories are merely tools—tentative guides—with which to begin observation and analysis. They are reassuring, however, to those who have low tolerance for ambiguity.

Defending the Qualitativeness of the Study

Frequently, in an attempt to make a proposed design efficient and conform to traditional research, reviewers recommend alterations in the original design. They may argue that the time for exploration is wasteful; they may try to change the nature of the study from ethnographic exploration and description to a more traditional design.

The following vignettes show how two different researchers developed rationales for their work. Vignette 25 describes how a proposal writer anticipated a funding agent's challenge to the usefulness of qualitative research. Vignette 26 shows how a doctoral student successfully withstood challenges to his right to alter the design during fieldwork if it became necessary or prudent.

Vignette 25

Justifying Time for Exploration

The proposal to conduct three in-depth case studies of high schools undergoing change (Rossman et al., 1984) had received favorable internal review, although one administrator made his standard objections about the value of qualitative research. The proposal had been transmitted to Washington, D.C., where it would receive close scrutiny as a major portion of the group's work scope over the next 5 years.

As the research team sat on the train heading south, they pondered the type of questions they would be required to answer. Surely their sampling plan would be challenged—the criterion of "improvement" would have to be quite broadly construed to locate the kinds of high schools they wanted. The notion of studying a school's culture was new to many in the research community, never mind Washington bureaucrats. The team anticipated questions about the usefulness of that concept, as well as the presentation of theoretical ideas on cultural change and transformation.

It struck the researchers as prudent to develop a rationale grounded in the applied research of others, rather than relying on anthropological constructs. As they reviewed that logic, three points seemed most salient. First, the research proposal assumed that change in schools cannot be adequately explored through a "snapshot" approach. Rather, the complexity of interactions among people, new programs, deeply held beliefs and values, and other organizational events demanded a long-term, in-depth approach. Second, at that time little was known about change processes in secondary schools. Most of the previous research focused on elementary schools and had been generalized, perhaps inappropriately, to secondary schools. The proposed research was intended to fill the gap. Finally, much had been written about teachers' resistance to change. The rationale for and significance of the study would be in uncovering some of that construct, in delving beneath the surface and exploring the meaning perspectives of teachers involved in profound change.

The proposal called for long-term engagement in the social worlds of the three high schools selected for study. The team anticipated a challenge to that time allocation and decided to defend it through the rationale presented above as well as with the idea that complex processes demand adequate time for exploration, that interactions and changes in belief systems occur slowly.

After the 2-hour hearing the team felt it had done a credible job, but realized that the funding agent had not yet come to accept the longer time frame of qualitative research. In the negotiations, the research team had had to modify the original plan to engage in participant observation over the course of a school year. To save the project from denial, they had agreed to 6 months of data collection, over the winter and spring terms.

In Vignette 25, the researchers had developed a sound logic for the major aspects of the study. Justification for the substantive focus grew from the conceptual framework and the significance of the study. The major research approach—long-term engagement in the social world—can best be justified through demonstrating the need for exploration. This is the hardest aspect to convince the critic about, as well as a crucial aspect of qualitative research. The next vignette shows how a doctoral student in economics successfully countered challenges to the need for design flexibility.

Vignette 26

Defending Flexibility [2]

Katz had been fascinated with families' financial decisions long before he first took a course in microeconomics as a college sophomore. That exposure to theory crystallized his interest and gave it an intellectual home. During his doctoral course work, however, he had pursued this interest from a cross-cultural perspective, enrolling in as many anthropology courses as his adviser would permit.

Katz's interest in the family's fiscal decision making grew as he read case studies of families in other cultures. Quite naturally, he became interested in the methods anthropologists used to gather their data; they seemed so very different from econometrics or even economic history methods. As he immersed himself in the classroom, his fascination grew. Now, about to embark on his dissertation, he had convinced one committee member to support his proposal to engage in a long-term, in-depth study of five families in very different socioeconomic circumstances. As he prepared for a meeting with the other two committee members, he reviewed the strengths of his proposal.

First, he was exploring the inner decision-making processes of five families—something no economics research had as yet done. The value of the research would rest, in part, on the contribution this would make to understanding the beliefs, values, and motivations of certain financial behaviors. Second, he was contributing to methodology because he was approaching a topic using new research methods. He could rely on the work of two or three other qualitative economists—well-established scholars in their fields—to demonstrate that others had undertaken such risky business and survived!

Third, he had thoroughly combed the methodological literature for information that would demonstrate his knowledge of many issues that would arise: The design section of the proposal was more than 60 pages long and addressed every conceivable issue. He had not attempted to resolve issues, but rather to show that he was aware that they might arise, knowledgeable about how others had dealt with the issues, and sensitive to the trade-offs represented by various decisions.

During the committee meeting, the thoroughness and richness of the design section served him well. The fully documented topics and sensitive discussion revealed a knowledge and sophistication not often found in doctoral students. What Katz had not anticipated, however, was the larger question brought up by one committee member: With such a small sample, how could the research be useful?

Fortunately, Katz recalled the argument developed by Kennedy (1979) about generalizing from single case studies. He had conceptualized his study as a set of family life histories from which would be drawn analytic categories, with relationships among them carefully delimited. Not unlike a multisite case study, Katz's proposal could be evaluated from that perspective. This logic proved sufficiently convincing that Katz's committee approved his proposal.

In the foregoing vignettes, each proposal demanded a well-thought-out, thorough, logical defense. When considered as an argument in support of the proposal, the need to develop a clear organization, build documentation for major design decisions, and demonstrate the overall soundness of the study as conceived becomes more clear. Following the advice provided in this book will help the qualitative research proposal writer to think through the conceptual and methodological justifications and rationales for the proposed study.

A Final Word

The process of developing a qualitative research proposal, the revisions necessitated by the interrelatedness of the sections, will create a final product that convinces readers and develops a rationale for the researcher's own guidance. It will justify the selection of qualitative methods and demonstrate the researcher's ability to conduct the research. The writing and creative processes will force the researcher to develop a research logic and plan that will guide and direct the research. The time, thought, and energy expended in writing a proposal that is theoretically sound, methodologically efficient, and thorough, and that demonstrates the researcher's capacity to conduct the research; to draw sound, credible, and convincing conclusions; and to write the final report will reap rewards throughout the research endeavor.

Notes

———

1. To avoid both sexist language and awkward constructions, we alternate use of feminine and masculine pronouns by paragraph throughout the text.

2. Vignettes are used as a heuristic device throughout the book. Many are based on our own work or the work of other researchers. Some are fictitious. Where a vignette is fictitious, we so indicate with a superscripted 2.

References

Alvarez, R. (1993). *Computer mediated communications: A study of the experience of women managers using electronic mail.* Unpublished manuscript, University of Massachusetts, Amherst.

Alwin, D. (1978). *Survey design and analysis.* Beverly Hills, CA: Sage.

Anderson, E. (1976). *A place on the corner.* Chicago: University of Chicago Press.

Anderson, G. (1989). Critical ethnography in education: Origins, current status, and new directions. *Review of Educational Research, 59,* 249-270.

Anthony, P. G., & Rossman, G. B. (1991). Evaluation proposal for *Restructuring for the integration of all students.* Malden: Massachusetts Department of Education, Office of Planning, Research, and Evaluation.

Asch, T. (Producer). (1970). *The feast* [Film]. Washington, DC: U.S. National Audiovisual Center.

Atkinson, P., Delamont, S., & Hammersley, M. (1988). Qualitative research traditions: A British response to Jacob. *Review of Educational Research, 58,* 231-250.

Bargar, R. R., & Duncan, J. K. (1982). Cultivating creative endeavor in doctoral research. *Journal of Higher Education, 53,* 1-31.

Barker, R. G. (1968). *Ecological psychology.* Stanford, CA: Stanford University Press.

Barzun, J., & Graff, H. F. (1970). *The modern researcher.* New York: Harcourt, Brace & World.

Becker, H. S., & Geer, B. (1969). Participant observation and interviewing: A comparison. In G. J. McCall & J. L. Simmons (Eds.), *Issues in participant observation: A text and reader* (pp. 322-331). Reading, MA: Addison-Wesley.

Becker, T. M., & Meyers, P. R. (1974-1975, Winter). Empathy and bravado: Interviewing reluctant bureaucrats. *Public Opinion Quarterly, 38,* 605-613.

Belson, W. A. (1982). *The design and understanding of survey questions.* Hants, UK: Gower.

Benbow, J. T. (1994). *Coming to know: A phenomenological study of individuals actively committed to radical social change.* Unpublished doctoral dissertation, University of Massachusetts, Amherst.

Benson, D. K., & Benson, J. L. (1975). *A guide to survey research teams.* Columbus, OH: Benchmark.

Berelson, B. (1952). *Content analysis in communication research.* Glencoe, IL: Free Press.

Berman, P. W., & Smith, V. L. (1984). Gender and situational differences in children's smiles, touches, and proxemics. *Sex Roles, 10,* 347-356.

Birdwhistell, R. L. (1970). *Kinesics and content: Essays on body motion communication.* Philadelphia: University of Pennsylvania Press.

Birn, R., Hague, P., & Vangelder, P. (1990). *A handbook of market research.* London: Routledge & Kegan Paul.

Blumer, H. (1969). *Symbolic interactionism.* Englewood Cliffs, NJ: Prentice Hall.

Blurton-Jones, N. (1972). *Ethnological studies of child behavior.* New York: Cambridge University Press.

Bogdan, R. C., & Biklen, S. K. (1992). *Qualitative research in education: An introduction to theory and methods* (2nd ed.). Boston: Allyn & Bacon.

Bogdan, R. C., & Taylor, S. (1975). *Introduction to qualitative research methods: A phenomenological approach to the social sciences.* New York: John Wiley.

Bowen, E. S. (1964). *Return to laughter.* Garden City, NY: Doubleday.

Bronfenbrenner, U. (1980). Ecology of childhood. *School Psychology Review, 9,* 294-297.

Brooks, P. C. (1969). *The use of unpublished primary sources.* Chicago: University of Chicago Press.

Bull, P. (1983). *Body movement and interpersonal communication.* New York: John Wiley.

Campbell, A. (1984). *The girls in the gang: A report from New York City.* New York: Basil Blackwell.

Chessman, C. (1954). *Cell 2455 death row.* Englewood Cliffs: NJ: Prentice Hall.

Chodorow, N. (1978). *The reproduction of mothering: Psychoanalysis and the sociology of gender.* Berkeley: University of California Press.

Christensen, H. T. (1960). Cultural relativism and premarital sex norms. *American Sociological Review, 25,* 31-39.

Christman, J. (1987). *Making both count: An ethnographic study of family and work in the lives of returning women graduate students.* Unpublished doctoral dissertation, University of Pennsylvania.

Clark, B. R. (1970). *The distinctive college: Antioch, Reed, and Swarthmore.* Chicago: Aldine.

Clarricoates, K. (1980). The importance of being Ernest, Emma, Tom, Jane. In R. Deem (Ed.), *Schooling for women's work* (pp. 26-41). London: Falmer.

Clarricoates, K. (1987). Child culture at school: A clash between gendered worlds? In A. Pollard (Ed.), *Children and their primary schools* (pp. 188-206). London: Falmer.

Cohen, S. L., & Fredler, J. E. (1974). Content analysis of multiple messages in suicide notes. *Life-threatening Behavior, 4,* 75-95.

Coles, R. (1971). *Children of crisis: Vol. 2, Migrants, sharecroppers, mountaineers.* Boston: Little, Brown.

Coles, R. (1977). *Privileged ones: The well-off and the rich in America.* Boston: Little, Brown.

Collier, J., & Collier, M. (1986). *Visual anthropology: Photography as a research method.* Albuquerque: University of New Mexico Press.

Connelly, F. M., & Clandinin, D. J. (1990). Stories of experience and narrative inquiry. *Educational Researcher, 19,* 2-14.

Cooper, H. M. (1988). Organizing knowledge syntheses: A taxonomy of literature reviews. *Knowledge in Society, 1,* 104-126.

156

Corbett, H. D., Dawson, J. L., & Firestone, W. A. (1984). *School context and school change.* New York: Teachers College Press.

Cormier, D. T. (1993). *Gilligan's theory extended: A case study of organizational conflict.* Unpublished doctoral dissertation, University of Massachusetts, Amherst.

Crane, D. R., & Griffin, W. (1983). Personal space: An objective measure of marital quality. *Journal of Mental and Family Therapy, 9,* 325-327.

Crites, S. (1986). Storytime: Recollecting the past and projecting the future. In T. R. Sarbin (Ed.), *Narrative psychology: The storied nature of human conduct* (pp. 152-173). New York: Praeger.

Davis, A., Gardner, B. B., & Gardner, M. R. (1941). *Deep South: A social anthropological study of caste and class.* Chicago: University of Chicago Press.

Day, D. E., Perkins, E. P., & Weinthaler, J. A. (1979). Naturalistic evaluation for program improvement. *Young Children, 34,* 12-24.

Denzin, N. K. (1970). *The research act: A theoretical introduction to sociological methods.* New York: McGraw-Hill.

Denzin, N. K., (1978). *The research act: A theoretical introduction to sociological methods* (2nd ed.). New York: McGraw-Hill.

Dobbert, M. L. (1982). *Ethnographic research: Theory and application for modern schools and societies.* New York: Praeger.

Dollard, J. (1935). *Criteria for the life history.* New Haven, CT: Yale University Press.

Douglas, J. D. (1976). *Investigative social research: Individual and team field research.* Beverly Hills, CA: Sage.

Edgerton, B. (1979). *Alone together.* Berkeley: University of California Press.

Edgerton, R. T., & Langness, L. L. (1974). *Methods and styles in the study of culture.* San Francisco: Chandler & Sharp.

Eisner, E. W. (1988). The primacy of experience and the politics of method. *Educational Researcher, 20,* 15-20.

Eisner, E. W. (1991). *The enlightened eye: Qualitative inquiry and the enhancement of educational practice.* New York: Macmillan.

Emerson, R. (1983). Introduction. In R. Emerson (Ed.), *Contemporary field research: A collection of readings* (pp. 255-268). Prospect Heights, IL: Waveland.

Erickson, F. (1977). Some approaches to inquiry in school-community ethnography. *Anthropology and Education Quarterly, 8,* 58-69.

Erickson, F., & Mahatt, G. (1982). Cultural organization of participation structures in two classrooms of Indian students. In G. Spindler (Ed.), *Doing the ethnography of schooling* (pp. 132-174). New York: Holt, Rinehart & Winston.

Erickson, F., & Wilson, J. (1982). *Sights and sounds of life in schools: A resource guide to film and videotape for research and education* (Research Series No. 125). East Lansing: Michigan State University, Institute for Research on Teaching.

Everhart, R. B. (1977). Between stranger and friend: Some consequences of "long-term" fieldwork in schools. *American Educational Research Journal, 14,* 1-15.

Evertson, C., & Green, J. (1985). Observation as inquiry and method. In M. C. Wittrock (Ed.), *Handbook of research on teaching* (pp. 162-213). New York: Macmillan.

Filstead, W. (Ed.). (1970). *Qualitative methodology.* Chicago: Markham.

Fischer, D. H. (1970). *Historians' fallacies: Toward a logic of historical thought.* New York: Harper & Row.

Freedman, J. (1975). *Crowding and behavior.* New York: Viking.

Friedan, B. (1981). *The second stage.* New York: Summit.

Friere, P. (1970). *Pedagogy of the oppressed.* New York: Seabury.

Funkhouser, G. R. (1973). The issues of the sixties: An exploratory study. *Public Opinion Quarterly, 37,* 62-75.

Galliher, J. F. (1983). Social scientists' ethical responsibilities to superordinates: Looking up meekly. In R. Emerson (Ed.), *Contemporary field research: A collection of readings* (pp. 300-311). Prospect Heights, IL: Waveland.

Gardner, R. (1974). *Rivers of sand* [Film]. New York: Phoenix Films.

Geer, B. (1969). First days in the field. In G. McCall & J. L. Simmons (Eds.), *Issues in participant observation* (pp. 144-162). Reading, MA: Addison-Wesley.

Geertz, C. (1973). Thick description: Toward an interpretive theory of culture. In C. Geertz (Ed.), *The interpretation of cultures: Selected essays* (pp. 3-30). New York: Basic Books.

Geertz, C. (1988). *Works and lives: The anthropologist as author.* Palo Alto, CA: Stanford University Press.

Giele, J. L. (Ed.). (1982). *Women in the middle years: Current knowledge and directions for research and policy.* New York: John Wiley.

Gilligan, C. (1982a). Adult development and women's development: Arrangements for a marriage. In J. Z. Giele (Ed.), *Women in the middle years: Current knowledge and directions for research and policy.* New York: John Wiley.

Gilligan, C. (1982b). *In a different voice: Psychological theory and women's development.* Cambridge, MA: Harvard University Press.

Glaser, B., & Strauss, A. (1967). *The discovery of grounded theory.* Chicago: Aldine.

Glesne, C. (1989). Rapport and friendship in ethnographic research. *Qualitative studies in education, 2,* 43-54.

Glesne, C., & Peshkin, A. (1992). *Becoming qualitative researchers: An introduction.* White Plains, NY: Longman.

Goffman, E. (1959). *The presentation of self in everyday life.* Garden City, NY: Doubleday Anchor.

Goode, W. J. (1960). Theory of role strain. *American Sociological Review, 25,* 483-496.

Goodenough, W. (1971). *Culture, language, and society.* Reading, MA: Addison-Wesley.

Gottschalk, L. A. (1969). *Understanding history.* New York: Knopf.

Gottschalk, L. A. (1979). *The content analysis of verbal behavior: Further studies.* New York: Spectrum.

Greenberg, B. S. (1980). *Life on television: Content analysis of U.S. TV drama.* Norwood, NJ: Ablex.

Griffin, C. (1985). *Typical girls?* London: Routledge & Kegan Paul.

Greene, J. C., Caracelli, V. J., & Graham, W. F. (1989). Towards a conceptual framework for mixed-methods evaluation design. *Educational Evaluation and Policy Analysis, 11,* 255-274.

Greenwald, J. (1992). *Environmental attitudes: A structural developmental model.* Unpublished doctoral dissertation, University of Massachusetts, Amherst.

Grumet, M. R. (1988). *Bitter milk: Women and teaching.* Amherst: University of Massachusetts Press.

Guba, E. G. (1978). *Toward a methodology of naturalistic inquiry in educational evaluation* (Monograph 8). Los Angeles: UCLA Center for the Study of Evaluation.

Hall, E. T. (1966). *The hidden dimension.* Garden City, NY: Doubleday.

Hall, E. T., & Hall, M. R. (1977). Nonverbal communication for educators. *Theory Into Practice, 16,* 141-144.

Hammersley, M. (1977). School learning: The cultural resources required to answer a teacher's question. In P. Woods & M. Hammersley (Eds.), *School experience* (pp. 58-86). London: Croom Helm.

158

Harding, S. (Ed.). (1987). *Feminism and methodology.* Bloomington: Indiana University Press.

Hargreaves, D. H. (1984). Teachers' questions: Open, closed, and half-open. *Educational Research, 26,* 46-52.

Herriott, R. E., & Firestone, W. A. (1983). Multisite qualitative policy research: Optimizing description and generalizability. *Educational Researcher, 12,* 14-19.

Hinton, B. E. (1985). Selected nonverbal communication factors influencing adult behavior and learning. *Lifelong Learning, 8,* 23-26.

Hockings, P. (Ed.). (1975). *Principles of visual anthropology.* Chicago: Aldine.

Hoffman, B. (1972). *Albert Einstein: Creator and rebel.* New York: Viking.

Hollingshead, A. B. (1975). *Elmtown's youth and Elmtown revisited.* New York: John Wiley.

Hollingsworth, S. (1991). *Narrative analysis on literacy education: A story of changing classrooms* (Research Series 202). East Lansing, MI: Institute for Research on Teaching.

Home Box Office Project Knowledge. (1992). *Educating Peter* [Film]. New York: Ambrose Video Publishing (Distributors).

Jackson, B. (1978). Killing time: Life in the Arkansas penitentiary. *Qualitative sociology, 1,* 21-32.

Jacob, E. (1987). Qualitative research traditions: A review. *Review of Educational Research, 51,* 1-50.

Jacob, E. (1988). Clarifying qualitative research: A focus on traditions. *Educational Researcher, 17,* 16-24.

Jick, T. D. (1979). Mixing qualitative and quantitative methods: Triangulation in action. *Administrative Science Quarterly, 24,* 602-661.

Jorgensen, D. L. (1989). *Participant observation: A methodology for human studies.* Newbury Park, CA: Sage.

Kahn, A. (1992). *Therapist initiated termination to psychotherapy: The experience of clients.* Unpublished doctoral dissertation, University of Massachusetts, Amherst.

Kahn, R., & Cannell, C. (1957). *The dynamics of interviewing.* New York: John Wiley.

Kalnins, Z. G. (1986, September). *An exploratory study of the meaning of life as described by residents of a long-term care facility.* Project proposal, Peabody College of Vanderbilt University, Nashville.

Kanter, R. (1977). *Men and women of the corporation.* New York: Basic Books.

Kaplan, A. (1964). *The conduct of inquiry.* San Francisco: Chandler.

Keddie, N. (1971). Classroom knowledge. In M.F.D. Young (Ed.), *Knowledge and control* (pp. 133-160). London: Collier-Macmillan.

Keiser, R. L. (1969). Cupid's story. In R. L. Keiser, *The vice lords: Warriors of the street.* New York: Holt, Rinehart & Winston.

Kemmis, S., & McTaggert, R. (Eds.). (1982). *The action research reader.* Geelong, Victoria, Australia: Deakin University Press.

Kennedy, M. M. (1979). Generalizing from single case studies. *Evaluation Quarterly, 12,* 661-678.

Krieger, S. (1985). Beyond "subjectivity": The use of the self in social science. *Qualitative Sociology, 8,* 309-324.

Krueger, R. A. (1988). *Focus groups: A practical guide for applied research.* Newbury Park, CA: Sage.

Lather, P. (1991). *Getting smart: Feminist research and pedagogy with/in the post modern.* London: Routledge & Kegan Paul.

Lawless, E. J. (1991). Methodology and research notes: Women's life stories and reciprocal ethnography as feminist and emergent. *Journal of Folklore Research, 28,* 35-60.

Lees, S. (1986). *Losing out.* London: Hutchinson.

Lesko, N. (1988). *Symbolizing society: Stories, rites and structure in a Catholic high school.* New York: Falmer.

Lewin, K. (1936). *Principles of ecological psychology.* New York: McGraw-Hill.

Libby, W. (1922). The scientific imagination. *Scientific Monthly, 15,* 263-270.

Lincoln, Y., & Guba, E. (1985). *Naturalistic inquiry.* Beverly Hills, CA: Sage.

Locke, L. F., Spirduso, W. W., & Silverman, S. J. (1993). *Proposals that work: A guide for planning dissertations and grant proposals* (3rd ed.). Newbury Park, CA: Sage.

Loughlin, C. F., & Suina, J. H. (1983). Reflecting the child's community in the classroom environment. *Childhood Education, 60,* 18-21.

Luckenbill, D. F. (1981). Researching murder transactions. In T. C. Wagenaar (Ed.), *Readings for social research.* Belmont, CA: Wadsworth.

Lutz, F., & Iannaccone, L. (1969). *Understanding educational organizations: A field study approach.* Columbus, OH: Charles Merrill.

Maddock, R., Kenny, C. T., Lupfer, M. B., & Rosen, C. V. (1977). A nonreactive measure of lost time among employees. *Journal of Psychology, 92,* 199-203.

Maguire, P. (1987). *Doing participatory research: A feminist approach.* Amherst, MA: Center for International Education.

Mandelbaum, D. G. (1973). The study of life history: Gandhi. *Current Anthropology, 14,* 177-207.

Manning, P. K. (1972). Observing the police: Deviants, respectables, and the law. In J. Douglas (Ed.), *Research on deviance* (pp. 213-268). New York: Random House.

Marshall, C. (1979). *Career socialization of women in school administration.* Unpublished doctoral dissertation, University of California, Santa Barbara.

Marshall, C. (1981). Organizational policy and women's socialization in administration. *Urban Education, 16,* 205-231.

Marshall, C. (1984). Elites, bureaucrats, ostriches, and pussycats: Managing research in policy settings. *Anthropology and Education Quarterly, 15,* 235-251.

Marshall, C. (1985a). Appropriate criteria of trustworthiness and goodness for qualitative research on education organizations. *Quality and Quantity, 19,* 353-373.

Marshall, C. (1985b). Field studies and educational administration and policy: The fit, the challenge, the benefits, and costs. *Urban Education, 20,* 61-81.

Marshall, C. (1985c). The stigmatized woman: The professional woman in a male sex-typed career. *Journal of Educational Administration, 23,* 131-152.

Marshall, C. (1986). *Power language and women's access to organizational leadership.* Grant proposal to the University Research Council, Vanderbilt University, Nashville.

Marshall, C. (1987, March 24). *Report to the Vanderbilt Policy Education Committee.* Vanderbilt University, Nashville.

Marshall, C. (1990). Goodness criteria: Are they objective or judgment calls? In E. Guba (Ed.), *The paradigm dialog* (pp. 188-197). Newbury Park, CA: Sage.

Marshall, C. (1991). Educational policy dilemmas: Can we have control and quality and choice and democracy and equity? In K. M. Borman, P. Swami, & L. D. Wagstaff (Eds.), *Contemporary issues in U.S. education.* Norwood, NJ: Ablex.

Marshall, C. (1992). School administrators' values: A focus on atypicals. *Educational Administration Quarterly, 28,* 368-386.

Marshall, C., Mitchell, D., & Wirt, F. (1985). Assumptive worlds of education policy makers. *Peabody Journal of Education, 6,* 90-115.

Marshall, C., Mitchell, D., & Wirt, F. (1986). The context of state level policy formulation. *Educational Evaluation and Policy Analysis, 8,* 347-378.

Massachusetts Department of Education. (1990, May). *Restructuring for the integration of all students*. Malden, MA: Office of Planning, Research and Evaluation.

Massachusetts Department of Education. (1990, November). Request for proposals for an evaluation of *Restructuring for the integration of all students*. Malden, MA: Office of Planning, Research and Evaluation.

McCall, G., & Simmons, J. L. (Eds.). (1969). *Issues in participant observation: A text and reader*. Reading, MA: Addison-Wesley.

McCracken, G. (1988). *The long interview*. Newbury Park, CA: Sage.

McKernan, J. (1991). *Curriculum action research: A handbook of methods and resources for the reflective practitioner*. London: Routledge & Kegan Paul.

Mead, M. (1970). The art and technology of fieldwork. In R. Narroll & R. Cohen (Eds.), *A handbook of method in cultural anthropology* (pp. 246-265). Garden City, NY: Natural History.

Metz, M. H. (1978). *Classrooms and corridors. The crisis of authority in desegregated secondary schools*. Berkeley: University of California Press.

Miles, M. S., & Huberman, A. M. (1984). *Qualitative data analysis: A sourcebook of new methods*. Beverly Hills, CA: Sage.

Miles, M. S., & Huberman, A. M. (1993). *Qualitative data analysis: A sourcebook of new methods* (2nd ed.). Newbury Park, CA: Sage.

Minister, K. (1991). A feminist frame for the oral history interview. In S. B. Gluck & D. Patai (Eds.), *Women's words: The feminist practice of oral history* (pp. 27-41). New York: Routledge & Kegan Paul.

Mitchell, D., Wirt, F., & Marshall, C. (1986). *Alternative state policy mechanisms for pursuing educational quality, equity, efficiency, and choice*. Final report to the U.S. Department of Education, grant no. NIE-G-83 0020.

Mitchell, W. J. (Ed.). (1981). *On narrative*. Chicago: University of Chicago Press.

Mooney, R. L. (1951). Problems in the development of research men. *Educational Research Bulletin, 30*, 141-150.

Morgan, D. L. (1988). *Focus groups as qualitative research*. Newbury Park, CA: Sage.

Naroll, R., & Cohen, R. (Eds.). (1970). *A handbook of method in cultural anthropology*. Garden City, NY: Natural History.

Olesen, V., & Whittaker, E. (1967a). Role-making in participant observation: Processes in the research-actor relationship. *Human Organization, 26*, 273-281.

Olesen, V., & Whittaker, E. (1967b). *The silent dialogue*. San Francisco: Jossey-Bass.

Oliver, K. (1990). *The lives of mothers following the death of a child: Toward an understanding of maternal bereavement*. Unpublished doctoral dissertation, University of Massachusetts, Amherst.

Patton, M. Q. (1980). *Qualitative evaluation methods*. Beverly Hills, CA: Sage.

Patton, M. Q. (1990). *Qualitative research and evaluation methods* (2nd ed.). Newbury Park, CA: Sage.

Pearsol, J. (1985, April). *Controlling qualitative data: Understanding teachers' value perspectives on a sex equity education project*. Paper presented at the annual meetings of the American Educational Research Association, Chicago.

Pelto, P., & Pelto, G. H. (1978). *Anthropological research: The structure of inquiry* (2nd ed.). New York: Cambridge University Press.

Peshkin, A. (1988). In search of subjectivity—one's own. *Educational Researcher, 17*, 17-21.

Piotrkowski, C. S. (1979). *Work and the family system. A naturalistic study of working-class and lower-middle-class families*. New York: Free Press.

Pleck, E. (1976). Two worlds in one: Work and family. *Journal of Social History, 70*, 178-195.

Platt, J. (1981). On interviewing one's peers. *British Journal of Sociology, 32*, 75-85.

Polkinghorne, D. E. (1988). *Narrative knowing and the human sciences.* Albany, NY: SUNY Press.

Polsky, N. (1969). *Hustlers, beats, and others.* Garden City, NY: Doubleday Anchor.

Powdermaker, H. (1966). *Stranger and friend.* New York: Norton.

Punch, M. (1986). *The politics and ethics of fieldwork.* Beverly Hills, CA: Sage.

Qualis Research Associates. (1987). *The ethnograph* [Computer program]. Littleton, CO: Author.

Rist, R. (1981, April). *Is there life after research? Ethical issues in the study of schools.* Paper presented at the annual meetings of the American Educational Research Association, Los Angeles.

Rizzuto, A. (1979). *The birth of a living God: A psychoanalytic study.* Chicago: University of Chicago Press.

Rollwagen, J. (Ed.). (1988). *Anthropological filmmaking.* New York: Harwood Academic Publishers.

Ross, M., & Conway, M. (1986). Remembering one's own past: The construction of personal histories. In R. Sorrentino & E. T. Higgins (Eds.), *Handbook of motivation and cognition: Foundations of social behavior* (pp. 122-144). New York: Guilford.

Rossman, G. B. (1984). I owe you one: Notes on role and reciprocity in a study of graduate education. *Anthropology and Education Quarterly, 15,* 225-234.

Rossman, G. B. (1985, April). *Studying professional cultures in improving high schools.* Paper presented at the annual meetings of the American Educational Research Association, Chicago.

Rossman, G. B., Corbett, H. D., & Dawson, J. L. (1986). Intentions and impacts: A comparison of sources of influence on local school systems. *Urban Education, 21,* 86-106.

Rossman, G. B., Corbett, H. D., & Firestone, W. A. (1984). *Plan for the study of professional cultures in improving high schools.* Philadelphia: Research for Better Schools.

Rossman, G. B., Corbett, H. D., & Firestone, W. A. (1988). *Change and effectiveness in schools: A cultural perspective.* Albany: SUNY Press.

Rossman, G. B., & Wilson, B. L. (1985). Numbers and words: Combining quantitative and qualitative methods in a single large-scale evaluation study. *Evaluation Review, 9,* 627-643.

Rossman, G. B., & Wilson, B. L. (1994). Numbers and words revisited: Being "shamelessly eclectic." *Quality and Quantity, 28,* 315-327.

Rossman, G. B., Wilson, B. L., & Corbett, H. D., (1985). *A cultural perspective on the local implementation of state school improvement programs* (Research proposal submitted to Florida State University). Philadelphia: Research for Better Schools.

Rutter, D. R. (1984). *Aspects of nonverbal communication.* Amsterdam: Swets & Zeitlinger.

Ryave, A. L., & Schenkein, J. N. (1974). Notes on the art of walking. In R. Turner (Ed.), *Ethnomethodology* (pp. 265-274). Baltimore: Penguin.

Sanday, P. R. (1979). The ethnographic paradigm(s). *Administrative Science Quarterly, 24,* 527-538.

Sarbin, T. R. (Ed.). (1986). *Narrative psychology: The storied nature of human conduct.* New York: Praeger.

Schatzman, L., & Strauss, A. (1973). *Field research: Strategies for a natural sociology.* Englewood Cliffs, NJ: Prentice Hall.

Scheflen, A. E. (1976). *Human territories: How we behave in space-time.* Englewood Cliffs, NJ: Prentice Hall.

Schein, E. H. (1985). *Organizational culture and leadership.* San Francisco: Jossey-Bass.

Schwartz, H., & Jacobs, J. (1979). *Qualitative sociology: A method to the madness.* New York: Free Press.

Sechrest, L. (Ed.). (1979). *Unobtrusive measurement today.* San Francisco: Jossey-Bass.

Sharp, R., & Green, A. (1975). *Education and social control.* London: Routledge & Kegan Paul.

162

Smelser, N. J., & Erickson, E. H. (1980). *Themes of work and love in adulthood.* Cambridge, MA: Harvard University Press.

Smith, J. K. (1988, March). *Looking for the easy way out: The desire for methodological constraints in openly ideological research.* Paper presented at the annual conference of the American Educational Research Association, New Orleans.

Smith, L. (1971). *Anatomy of an educational innovation.* New York: John Wiley.

Smith, P. K. (1974). Ethnological methods. In B. Foss (Ed.), *New perspectives in child development* (pp. 85-137). Harmondsworth, UK: Penguin.

Soloway, I., & Walters, J. (1977). Workin' the corner: The ethics and legality of ethnographic fieldwork among active heroin addicts. In R. S. Weppner (Ed.), *Street ethnography* (pp. 159-178). Beverly Hills, CA: Sage.

Sorenson, E. R. (1968). The retrieval of data from changing cultures. *Anthropological Quarterly, 41,* 177-186.

Spradley, J. S. (1979). *The ethnographic interview.* New York: Holt, Rinehart & Winston.

Spradley, J. S. (1980). *Participant observation.* New York: Holt, Rinehart & Winston.

Sudman, S., & Bradburn, N. M. (1982). *Asking questions.* San Francisco: Jossey-Bass.

Sutherland, E. H., & Conwell, C. (1983). *The professional thief.* Chicago: University of Chicago Press.

Taylor, S. J., & Bogdan, R. (1984). *Introduction to qualitative research: The search for meanings* (2nd ed.). New York: John Wiley.

Tesch, R. (1990). *Qualitative research: Analysis types and software tools.* New York: Falmer.

Thomas, W. I. (1949). *Social structure and social theory.* New York: Free Press.

Thompson, E. (Ed.). (1939). *Race relations and the race problem.* Durham, NC: Duke University Press.

Thorne, B. (1983). Political activists as participant observer: Conflicts of commitment in a study of the draft resistance movement of the 1960s. In R. Emerson (Ed.), *Contemporary field research: A collection of readings* (pp. 216-234). Prospect Heights, IL: Waveland.

Tripp, D. H. (1983). Co-authorship and negotiation: The interview as act of creation. *Interchange, 14,* 32-45.

True, W. R., & True, J. H. (1977). Network analysis as a methodological approach to the study of drug use in a Latin city. In R. S. Weppner (Ed.), *Street ethnography* (pp. 125-141). Beverly Hills, CA: Sage.

Valli, L. (1986). *Becoming clerical workers.* New York: Routledge & Kegan Paul.

Van Maanen, J. (1983). The moral fix: On the ethics of fieldwork. In R. Emerson (Ed.), *Contemporary field research: A collection of readings* (pp. 269-287). Prospect Heights, IL: Waveland.

Van Maanen, J. (1988). *Tales of the field: On writing ethnography.* Chicago: University of Chicago Press.

Van Manen, M. (1990). *Researching lived experience: Human science for an action sensitive pedagogy.* Buffalo: SUNY Press.

Vidich, A. (1969). Participant observation and the collection and interpretation of data. In G. McCall & J. L. Simmons (Eds.), *Issues in participant observation* (pp. 78-87). Reading, MA: Addison-Wesley.

Viney, L. L., & Bousefield, L. (1991). Narrative analysis: A method of psychosocial research for AIDS-affected people. *Social Science and Medicine, 23,* 757-765.

Walker, R. (1983). The use of case studies in applied research and evaluation. In A. Hartnett (Ed.), *The social sciences and educational studies* (pp. 190-204). London: Heinemann.

Wax, M. L. (1983). On fieldworkers and those exposed to fieldwork: Federal regulations and moral issues. In R. Emerson (Ed.), *Contemporary field research: A collection of readings* (pp. 288-299). Prospect Heights, IL: Waveland.

Wax, R. (1971). *Doing fieldwork: Warnings and advice.* Chicago: University of Chicago Press.

Webb, E., Campbell, D. T., Schwartz, R. D., & Sechrest, L. (1966). *Unobtrusive measures: Nonreactive research in the social sciences.* Chicago: Rand McNally.

Webb, E., & Salancik, J. (1966). The interviewer or the only wheel in town. *Journalism Monograph, 2.*

Webb, E., & Weick, K. E. (1979). Unobtrusive measures in organizational theory: A reminder. *Administrative Science Quarterly, 24,* 650-659.

Webb, M. B. (1990). Listen and learn from narratives that tell a story. *Religious Education, 85,* 617-630.

Weick, K. E. (1976). Educational organizations as loosely coupled systems. *Administrative Science Quarterly, 21,* 1-19.

Westley, W. A. (1967). The police: Law, custom, and morality. In P. I. Rose (Ed.), *The study of society* (pp. 766-779). New York: Random House.

Whyte, W. F. (1955). *Street corner society.* Chicago: University of Chicago Press.

Whyte, W. H. (1980). *The social life of small urban spaces.* Washington: The Conservation Foundation.

Whyte, W. F. (1984). *Learning from the field: A guide from experience.* Beverly Hills, CA: Sage.

Wilson, S. (1977). The use of ethnographic techniques in educational research. *Review of Educational Research, 47,* 245-265.

Wiseman, F. (1969). *High school* [Film]. Boston: Zipporan Films.

Wolcott, H. F. (1985). On ethnographic intent. *Educational Administration Quarterly, 3,* 187-203.

Yablonsky, L. (1965). *The tunnel back: Synanon.* Baltimore, MD: Penguin.

Yin, R. K. (1984). *Case study research: Design and methods.* Beverly Hills, CA: Sage.

Young, M. F. D. (Ed.). (1971). *Knowledge and control.* London: Collier-Macmillan.

Zelditch, M. (1962). Some methodological problems of field studies. *American Journal of Sociology, 67,* 566-576.

Ziller, R. C., & Lewis, D. (1981). Orientations: Self, social and environmental precepts through auto-photography. *Personality and Social Psychology Bulletin, 7,* 338-343.

Author Index

Subject Index

List of Tables, Figures, and Vignettes

Tables

Figures

Vignettes

About the Authors

Catherine Marshall is Professor in the Department of Educational Leadership at the University of North Carolina at Chapel Hill. She received her Ph.D. from the University of California, Santa Barbara, benefited from a postdoctoral fellowship at UCLA, and served on the faculty of the University of Pennsylvania and Vanderbilt University before taking her current position at North Carolina. The ongoing goal of her teaching and research has been to use an interdisciplinary approach to analyze cultures of schools, state policy systems, and other organizations. She served as the editor of the *Peabody Journal of Education* and has published extensively about the politics of education, qualitative methodology, women's access to careers, and the socialization, language, and values in educational administration.

She is also author or editor of three other books. They are *Culture and Education Policy in the American States,* with Douglas Mitchell and Frederick Wirt; *The Assistant Principal: Leadership Choices and Challenges; The New Politics of Gender and Race* (editor); and *The Administrative Career: Cases for Entry, Equity, and Endurance.* Early in her scholarly career, while conducting qualitative research on policy and teaching literally hundreds of doctoral students how to adopt and adapt the qualitative approach into workable proposals, she recognized a need and began to develop this book.

Gretchen B. Rossman is Professor of Education and Director of the Center for Education Policy at the University of Massachusetts at Amherst. She received her Ph.D. in education from the University of Pennsylvania with a specialization in higher education administration. Prior to coming to the University of Massachusetts, she was Senior Research Associate at Research for Better Schools in Philadelphia. Her research has focused on the local impact of changes in federal, state, and local policy. Her current interests include studying school-based restructuring efforts to more fully include students with disabilities, as well as those served by Chapter 1 and bilingual education programs, in the regular classroom. Funded for 5 years, this current work has resulted in several publications and invitations to speak at national forums on inclusive education.

Her study of school cultures, *Change and Effectiveness in Schools: A Cultural Perspective,* written with Dick Corbett and Bill Firestone, was published in 1988. A second policy study, *Mandating Academic Excellence: High School Responses to State Curriculum Reform,* with Bruce Wilson, was published in 1993. In addition to her teaching and research responsibilities, she consults regularly on restructuring in schools and serves as a qualitative evaluation specialist to several educational organizations.